Contents

Little Cayman Dive Sites   88

Marine Life   102

Diving Conservation & Awareness   108

Listings   112

Index   122

Authors

Jean Pierce & Kris Newman

Jean, a divemaster, and Kris, a dive instructor, reside in Napa, California and maintain offices in the Napa Valley and in Southern California's Sun Valley. However, they're frequently on location with their company Reeldivers, providing underwater dive and marine support for film productions. They managed the dive unit for the Warner Brothers film *Sphere* for which Kris also trained the principal actors. Jean is an award-winning travel

journalist and board member of the Society of American Travel Writers. She was Senior Editor of Travel Guidebooks at Rand McNally Publishing Co., Editor-in-Chief for Simon & Schuster Travel Guides in Chicago and Editor of *Odyssey* magazine. Jean's love is now dive-travel writing and both Kris and Jean are avid underwater photojournalists.

From the Authors

We offer a warm *thank you* to our wonderful friends, Patty and Mike McClellan, who generously loaned us camera equipment and have served as invaluable safety divers on film productions. Another big thanks to Kent Michels, a great friend and willing model. For logistics in the Cayman Islands, we thank Lynda Long and the Cayman Islands Department of Tourism. For assistance on Cayman Brac, we thank Brac Aquatics & Photo Centre, Ian Stewart and the Brac Caribbean Beach Village. On Little Cayman, we're grateful to Chris and family at Sam McCoy's Diving Lodge and to Peter and Terry at the Southern Cross Club. We appreciate Grand Cayman assistance from Bob Soto's Diving and Ocean Frontiers; Treasure Island Resort; Doug Ehnes, Maurice "Mo" Fitzgerald, Ron Kipp, Dr. John Madden and Gina Ebanks-Petrie (Department of the Environment). For help with dive gear, we thank Oceanic and our good friend Jon Hayes; ScubaPro; and Bob Evans and Susan Chess who manufacture our favorite underwater footwear, Force Fins. For our photo equipment we appreciate help from Ikelite and from Sea & Sea, for loaning us their beautiful 12mm lens. And finally, we thank DEPP (Divers Equipment Protection Program) for giving us peace of mind while transporting all that valuable equipment.

Photography Notes

Authors Jean Pierce and Kris Newman shot most of the images used in this book. As a veteran travel writer, Jean's land-based photos have accompanied her book contributions and magazine stories spanning a period of almost 15 years. Now she particularly enjoys the thrill and challenges of underwater photography with husband Kris. Thomas Morrisey, co-member with Jean in the Society of American Travel Writers, contributed several of the book's images.

Steve Rosenberg, an award-winning photographer and author of two Pisces dive guides, contributed many of the photographs in this book. Other images were provided by Michael Lawrence, Steve Simonsen, Lawson Wood and Len Zell.

From the Publisher

This first edition was produced in Lonely Planet's U.S. office under direction from Roslyn Bullas, the Pisces Books publishing manager. Wendy Smith edited the book with invaluable contributions from Senior Editor Debra Miller and sharp-eyed proofreading from Kevin Anglin. Emily Douglas designed the book and cover. Patrick Bock and Guphy created the maps, which were adapted from the author's extensive base maps, under the supervision of Alex Guilbert, the U.S. office's cartography manager. Hayden Foell, Scott Summers and Bill Miller provided technical help for the illustration and cover image.

Lonely Planet Pisces Books

Lonely Planet acquired the Pisces line of diving and snorkeling books in 1997. The series is being developed and substantially revamped over the next few years. We welcome your comments and suggestions.

Pisces Pre-Dive Safety Guidelines

Before embarking on a scuba diving, skin diving or snorkeling trip, carefully consider the following to help ensure a safe and enjoyable experience:

- Possess a current diving certification card from a recognized scuba diving instructional agency (if scuba diving)
- Be sure you are healthy and feel comfortable diving
- Obtain reliable information about physical and environmental conditions at the dive site (e.g., from a reputable local dive operation)
- Be aware of local laws, regulations and etiquette about marine life and environment
- Dive at sites within your experience level; if possible, engage the services of a competent, professionally trained dive instructor or divemaster

Underwater conditions vary significantly from one region, or even site, to another. Seasonal changes can significantly alter site and dive conditions. These differences influence the way divers dress for a dive and what diving techniques they use.

There are special requirements for diving in any area, regardless of location. Before your dive, ask about environmental characteristics that can affect your diving and how trained local divers deal with these considerations.

Warning & Request

Things change—dive site conditions, regulations, topside information. Nothing stays the same for long. Your feedback on this book will be used to help update and improve the next edition. Excerpts from your correspondence may appear in *Planet Talk*, our quarterly newsletter, or *Comet*, our monthly email newsletter. Please let us know if you do not want your letter published or your name acknowledged.

Correspondence can be addressed to:
Lonely Planet Publications
Pisces Books
150 Linden Street
Oakland, CA 94607
email: pisces@lonelyplanet.com

Introduction

MICHAEL LAWRENCE

The Caribbean's tiny Cayman Islands maintain an impressive reputation in the diving world. Lush reefs and legendary walls, an extensive marine park system and fine-tuned dive operations have helped this British Crown colony to court divers and snorkelers successfully since the 1950s. Grand Cayman, Cayman Brac and Little Cayman, all perched atop a vast submarine mountain ridge, look down like regal monarchs upon the deepest water in the Caribbean—the awesome Cayman Trench. For divers, this means it takes just minutes to get from beach grass to abyss. With 265 moored sites and plenty of shore diving and snorkeling possibilities, a nondiving day is practically unheard of.

The principal island for commerce and tourism and a high-profile center for international offshore banking, Grand Cayman is a prosperous place. Caymanians, who number about 34,000 in Grand Cayman, pay no income or property taxes and enjoy a very high standard of living—among the highest in the world. Consequently, this is no budget diver's paradise. Visitors will find that prices are steep, especially for meals, and should plan their finances accordingly. Grand Cayman's West End is

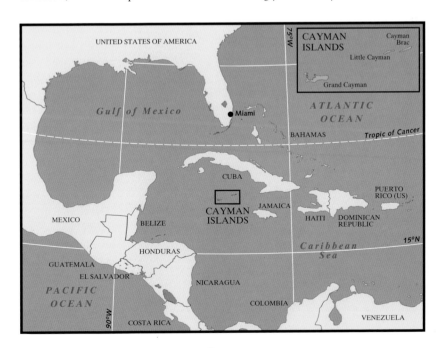

home to most of the island's dive operations. About 80% of the diving takes place on the West End, where weather conditions are consistently the best. Water and weather conditions are generally a bit rougher on Grand Cayman's East End, but adventurous divers are rewarded with pristine dive sites and a more authentic version of the local lifestyle.

Of the three islands, Cayman Brac is least affected by tourism. On "the Brac," as it's called locally, the population is small (about 1,500), so you can experience true island life—friendly, laid-back and slow-paced. Where else would you find street names like Bluff Boulevard and Mango Tree Road? The island's porous limestone is riddled with caves and the bluff is covered with an attractive combination of palms, cacti and bushes of yellow shamrock. Under the water, divers find a pristine reef and dive sites just minutes from shore.

Little Cayman is the most private and least developed of the Caymans. Permanent residents number fewer than 100, the airport runway is made of grass and gravel, and there's just one grocery store and a single restaurant. A bike is sufficient for transportation, but if you rent a car—yes, there's only one car rental agency—you're cautioned to brake for iguanas and ducks. "Development" here usually involves either installing new mooring buoys or repairing old ones. Known to bird-watchers as home to the largest breeding colony of red-footed

PIERCE & MORRISEY

Surface interval on Little Cayman.

booby birds in the Western Hemisphere, Little Cayman's claim to diving fame is the wall at Bloody Bay Marine Park, which sets the standard for extreme verticality underwater.

Three islands, three completely different temperaments—that's the attraction and the beauty. Choose any one of the islands for a terrific experience or, better yet, sample all three.

This book provides information for 56 of the best dive sites in the Cayman Islands, divided according to island. Information about location, depth range, access and expertise rating is provided for each site. You will also find detailed descriptions of each site, outlining conditions and noting topographical features and marine life you can expect to see. The Marine Life section provides a gallery of the Caymans' common fish and invertebrate life. Though this book is not intended to be a stand-alone travel guide, the Practicalities and Overview sections offer useful information about the islands, while the Activities & Attractions section provides ideas about how to spend your time above the water.

PIERCE & NEWMAN

Crowds are nonexistent at Little Cayman's resorts.

Overview

PIERCE & NEWMAN

No island in the Caribbean is more distant from its neighboring land masses than Grand Cayman, a fact that greatly influenced the islands' colonial development. While control of islands throughout the Caribbean passed back and forth among the colonial powers, the Cayman Islands remained relatively quiet, contained and politically stable. Today, this British outpost exudes order, efficiency and prosperity.

Just 460 miles (740km) south of Miami, Grand Cayman is the largest of the three islands—22 miles (35km) long and 7 miles (11km) wide. Cayman Brac and Little Cayman—the smaller "Sister Islands"— lie about 90 miles (145km) northeast of Grand Cayman. Twelve miles (19km) long and 1.5 miles (2.5km) wide, Cayman Brac has a distinctive central limestone bluff (*brac* is the Gaelic word for bluff) that begins on the West End and rises gradually as it extends eastward. It culminates on the East End in a sheer cliff rising 140ft (42m) above the sea. Little Cayman, the smallest of the islands, lies about a mile (1.6km) west of Cayman Brac. Slightly smaller than the Brac, Little Cayman is flat and its interior consists largely of saltwater ponds and dense mangrove forests.

History

In 1503, Christopher Columbus came upon the Cayman Islands accidentally, landing on what are now Little Cayman and Cayman Brac. At the time, both were uninhabited. He claimed them for Spain and named them Las Tortugas (The Turtles) for the large numbers of turtles he found. These huge sea turtles were coveted as meat for European sailors, so during the 16th, 17th and 18th centuries the islands became a replenishing center for merchant ships, explorers and buccaneers. The name Cayman is derived from the Carib word for the long-extinct marine crocodile—*caymanas*.

Spain never actually occupied the islands and in 1655 the British gained control. Fifteen years later the Cayman Islands, along with Jamaica, officially became part of the British Empire under the Treaty of Madrid. With the advent of royal land grants in 1734, settlers from England, Scotland and Wales began to settle in the islands. In some places, especially on the Sister Islands, you can still detect a Scottish brogue and will see family names like Kirkconnell and Tibbetts. For three centuries the islands were a dependency of Jamaica but all ties were severed in 1962 when Jamaica declared its independence from Britain.

Unlike in other parts of the Caribbean, slavery never played a major role in the Caymans, though the islands were situated along the slave route. With no sugar plantations or other significant agriculture, there was little demand for a labor pool. The first West Africans literally washed ashore from shipwrecks and by the late 1700s they made up more than half the Caymans' small population of fewer than 1,000. Emancipation came from Britain in 1835. Today, the islands are fully integrated and the population is a melting pot of islanders of European, West African, American and Jamaican descent.

Throughout the 1700s, the islands—particularly the nearly uninhabited Sister Islands—were notorious pirate lairs. Blackbeard (Edward Teach), Sir Henry Morgan and Anne Bonny were some of the legendary unsavory characters that preyed on ships traveling the commerce route between Jamaica and Central America. The British became increasingly frustrated by the loss of cargo and ships and mounted a bloody battle off the north coast of Little Cayman—the namesake for Bloody Bay Wall. By the mid-1700s, the British Royal Navy had finally swept pirates from the Caribbean altogether.

At the turn of the 19th century, a thriving shipbuilding industry developed, using mahogany and other local hardwoods. Still, the islands remained relatively isolated until the first wireless station was built in 1935.

Throughout the years, the Cayman Islands remained loyal to the British Crown, never experiencing the turbulent independence movements that happened in most of Britain's colonies in the West Indies. Today, only the Cayman Islands, Anguilla, Bermuda, the British Virgin Islands, Montserrat and the Turks & Caicos Islands remain true British Crown colonies. The designation British Crown colony indicates that these islands have a government of direct British rule, primarily through appointed, rather than elected, representatives.

The first significant influx of tourism came to the islands in 1953 with the construction of Grand Cayman's Owen Roberts International Airport. Four years later Bob Soto started the islands' first dive operation. Bob Soto was also one of the earliest local proponents of marine conservation and underwater parks. Dive travelers discovered the islands in the 1970s and Grand Cayman became one of the first warm-water vacation spots for

PIERCE & NEWMAN

The Union Jack waves proudly in this British Crown colony.

divers. Thereafter, thanks primarily to its sophisticated infrastructure—and the attractions bestowed by Mother Nature—divers began arriving in record numbers.

Offshore Rewards

In 1794, a landmark event dramatically affected the destiny of the Cayman Islands. As the story goes, 10 English merchant ships ran aground on the windy East End of Grand Cayman. Islanders were quick to act and managed to rescue all of the ships' passengers and crew. The English Crown expressed its gratitude in a sweeping gesture, declaring the Caymans forever free from taxation. The policy survives today—Cayman residents pay no income, property or capital gains taxes on money earned in the Cayman Islands.

The attractive tax situation drew banking and insurance businesses to the islands. This activity in turn stimulated the economy to such a degree that finance quickly replaced seafaring as the islands' major source of income. Over time, governmental and economic stability—as well as the implementation of strict confidentiality laws—have contributed to the Caymans' reputation as a major offshore banking center.

An offshore bank is loosely defined as a banking institution that serves foreign customers as its primary business. In general, offshore banking is characterized by

minimum governmental control, low taxes and notably high levels of privacy and confidentiality. Confidentiality laws modeled after those in Swiss banks assure investors that all financial dealings with persons in a position of trust—banks, brokerage firms, etc.—will never be disclosed without the investor's consent. So while many offshore investors are simply seeking secure investments without fear of currency control, others are mainly interested in anonymity and confidentiality—in short, they want to hide their money. And in general, if somebody's out to get someone else's money, they're not likely to track it down in the Cayman Islands. But *sssh*—we never told you that.

Visitors and investors are welcome.

Geography

Strange as it may seem, the Cayman Islands could be described as a tropical *mountain* paradise. The three tiny islands are actually exposed summits of the Cayman Ridge, an enormous subsea mountain range that extends from southeast Cuba nearly to Belize. Underwater, this translates into awesome wall diving. Some of these walls slope down at a gradual angle, while others are spectacularly vertical, plummeting straight into the depths. Moreover, this ridge forms the northern boundary of another equally amazing phenomenon—the Cayman Trench, also called the Bartlett Trough. This is the deepest part of the Caribbean Sea, with water depths of more than 4 miles (6km). North of the Cayman Ridge is the Yucatan Basin, with water depths of nearly 3 miles (4.5km).

In addition to these submarine cliffs, fringing coral reefs surround both Grand Cayman and Little Cayman, creating shallow lagoons. The lagoons consist primarily of rubble, sand and grass beds. Also surrounding each of the islands is a narrow, shallow shelf that hosts prolific coral communities. Generally, the shelf consists of two gently sloping terraces, with the deeper of these terraces featuring both spur-and-groove and patch reef coral systems. Spur-and-groove formations are characterized by coral fingers ("spurs")—which extend perpendicular from the shallow shoreline—separated by narrow sand-filled "grooves." Beyond the shelf begin the precipitous slopes of the Cayman Ridge. In Little Cayman's Bloody Bay, the two-tiered shelf configuration is notably different. Here, the shelves merge into a single vertical wall—a spectacular geologic development.

The walls' upper portions—from 50 to 100ft (15 to 30m)—feature abundant coral growth. Expect to find shingle-like star corals, as well as tube sponges and green and coralline algae. Below 80ft (24m) you'll begin to see caves, small cavities and ledges. Large basket, tube and rope sponges are common below the shelf break. Naturally, this grand undersea mountain range acts as a magnet to marine life.

On land, the limestone islands are ringed mostly by a craggy black ironshore coast, though in many places you'll find expanses of glistening white sand. Named for its dark color, ironshore is actually old coral that has been exposed to the elements—rainfall on the coral's calcium carbonate forms a mild carbonic acid, which eats away at the coral surface, leaving a dark, pockmarked rock-like surface.

PIERCE & MORRISEY

Find serenity and superb views on Cayman Brac's high bluff.

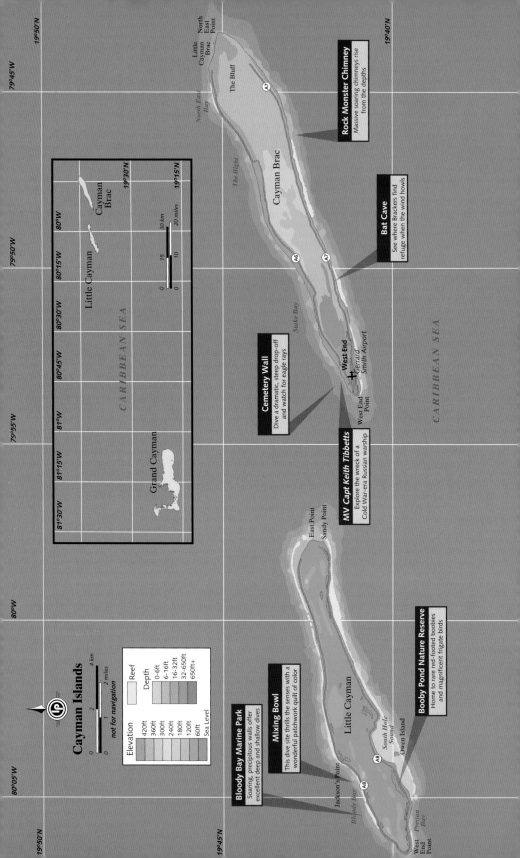

Cayman Islands

0   2   4 km
0   1   2 miles
not for navigation

Elevation

	420ft
	360ft
	300ft
	240ft
	180ft
	120ft
	60ft
	Sea Level

Reef

Depth

	0–6ft
	6–16ft
	16–32ft
	32–650ft
	650ft+

CARIBBEAN SEA

Grand Cayman

Little Cayman

Cayman Brac

81°30'W 81°15'W 81°W 80°45'W 80°30'W 80°15'W 80°W

19°30'N

19°15'N

0   15   30 km
0   10   20 miles

Bloody Bay Marine Park
Soaring, precipitous walls offer
excellent deep and shallow dives

Mixing Bowl
This dive site thrills the senses with a
wonderful patchwork quilt of color

Booby Pond Nature Reserve
Home to rare red-footed boobies
and magnificent frigate birds

Jackson's Point

Bloody Bay

West
End
Point

Preston
Bay

Little Cayman

South Hole
Sound

Owen Island

A8

A9

East Point

Sandy Point

MV Capt Keith Tibbetts
Explore the wreck of a
Cold War-era Russian warship

Cemetery Wall
Dive a dramatic, steep drop-off
and watch for eagle rays

West End
Point

West End

*Gerrard
Smith Airport*

Stake Bay

A6

A7

Bat Cave
See where Brackers find
refuge when the wind howls

A7

Cayman Brac

The Bight

CARIBBEAN SEA

Rock Monster Chimney
Massive soaring chimneys rise
from the depths

North East
Bay

The Bluff

A7

Little
Cayman
Brac

North
East
Point

19°50'N

19°45'N

80°05'W 80°W 79°55'W 79°50'W 79°45'W

19°50'N

19°40'N

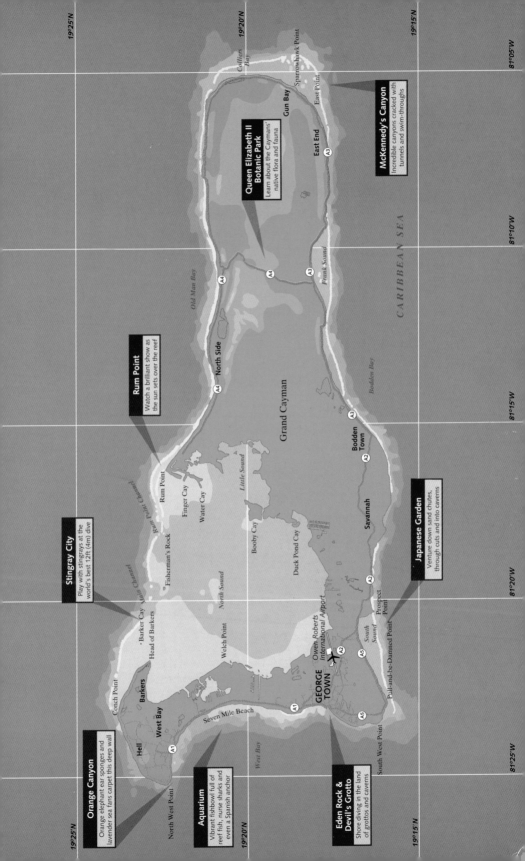

Orange Canyon
Orange elephant ear sponges and lavender sea fans carpet this deep wall

Stingray City
Play with stingrays at the world's best 12ft (4m) dive

Aquarium
Vibrant fishbowl full of reef fish, nurse sharks and even a Spanish anchor

Eden Rock & Devil's Grotto
Shore diving in the land of grottos and caverns

Rum Point
Watch a brilliant show as the sun sets over the reef

Queen Elizabeth II Botanic Park
Learn about the Caymans' native flora and fauna

McKennedy's Canyon
Incredible canyons cracked with tunnels and swim-throughs

Japanese Garden
Venture down sand chutes, through cuts and into caverns

19°25'N
19°20'N
19°15'N

81°05'W
81°10'W
81°15'W
81°20'W
81°25'W

Collier Bay
Sparrowhawk Point
Gun Bay
East Point
East End
Frank Sound
Boddon Bay
Old Man Bay
North Side
Bodden Town
Savannah
Prospect Point
Pull-and-be-Damned Point
South Sound
Owen Roberts International Airport
GEORGE TOWN
Seven Mile Beach
West Bay
South West Point
Hell
West Bay
North West Point
Conch Point
Barkers
Head of Barkers
Welch Point
Barker Cay
North Sound
Rum Point Channel
Main Channel
Fisherman's Rock
Rum Point
Finger Cay
Water Cay
Little Sound
Booby Cay
Duck Pond Cay

Grand Cayman

CARIBBEAN SEA

A1
A2
A3
A4
A5

Practicalities

PIERCE & NEWMAN

Climate

The Cayman Islands experience a tropical marine climate with warm, rainy summers (May to October) and cool, relatively dry winters (November to April). Average yearly rainfall is 60 inches (150cm) with March and April as the driest months. The rainy season starts in May and usually peaks in October, but showers rarely last more than a couple of hours. In the winter, air temperatures range from 70 to 80°F (21 to 27°C). In the summer, temperatures range from 80 to 90°F (27 to 32°C), but trade winds help keep the islands cool. Humidity levels vary from 68 to 92%. Summertime water temperatures average a steady 85°F (29°C), dropping to about 78°F (26°C) in winter. Generally, the Caribbean hurricane season is June through November. The Caymans are protected by large land masses in several directions—Cuba to the north, Haiti and the Dominican Republic to the east, Jamaica to the southeast and the Central American coastline to the west—so they tend to be protected from the worst storms and hurricanes. Still, hurricanes do strike and have caused tremendous damage.

Cayman water temperatures are bathtub-warm year-round.

Language

As a British dependency, the Caymans have English as the official language. You might detect a Gaelic brogue in some of the natives—it's a product of their Scottish heritage. Don't be surprised if you hear locals say CayMAN, with the accent on the second syllable—this is actually the correct pronunciation.

Getting There

Cayman Airways (☎ 949-2311) offers direct flights to Grand Cayman and Cayman Brac from U.S. gateway cities and has jet service from Grand Cayman to Cayman Brac. American Airlines, Delta, Northwest Airlines and US Air also fly to Grand Cayman from major U.S. cities. British Airways flies direct from London's Gatwick airport to Grand Cayman. Regular service from Jamaica is on Cayman Airways and Air Jamaica. Isleña Airlines flies out of La Ceiba, Honduras.

Island Air (☎ 949-0241), which uses small turbo-props, runs daily flights between Grand Cayman and the Sister Islands. This is the only type of service available to Little Cayman due to Little Cayman's grass landing strip. The flight between Grand Cayman and either of the Sister Islands is short, about 35 minutes. One important note: Island Air has a *strict* baggage limit of 55lbs (25kg) per person, which can present a problem for divers and underwater photographers. Not only will you have to pay extra for each pound over the weight limit, but your luggage might be put onto a different flight. There is no ferry service between the islands.

Many visitors to the Cayman Islands arrive as part of a cruise-ship itinerary. Most cruise ships depart from Miami, Tampa Bay or Fort Lauderdale. See the Listings section for information on major cruise lines serving the Cayman Islands.

Cruise ships bring thousands of visitors a year to Grand Cayman's George Town Harbour.

Gateway City - George Town

George Town, on Grand Cayman's West End, is the islands' capital and center of commerce. T-shirt shops mingle with multinational banks and duty-free stores, while cruise ships loom in the harbor. Stretching north from George Town is the tourist mecca called Seven Mile Beach, home to most of the island's resorts, restaurants, fast-food chains and shops.

PIERCE & NEWMAN
Locals clean the morning catch at George Town Harbour.

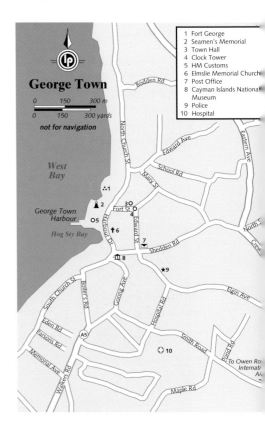

George Town

| 0 | 150 | 300 m |
| 0 | 150 | 300 yards |

not for navigation

1 Fort George
2 Seamen's Memorial
3 Town Hall
4 Clock Tower
5 HM Customs
6 Elmslie Memorial Church
7 Post Office
8 Cayman Islands National Museum
9 Police
10 Hospital

Getting Around

Grand Cayman has no airport shuttles, but taxis are plentiful. To really explore the island, you'll want to rent a car from one of the many agencies found at the airport, in George Town, along Seven Mile Beach and at many of the resorts. You'll need a temporary driver's license, which you can purchase when you rent the car. Driving in the Caymans is on the left side of the road—cars have the steering column on the right and those with stick shifts require shifting with the left hand, which can pose a challenge if you're not used to it.

On Cayman Brac, cabs are available at the airport in case your lodging doesn't pick you up. You can rent a car or a motor scooter at the airport or at other agencies around the island, but a bicycle (available from most resorts) might be sufficient.

When you arrive on Little Cayman, your resort will arrange to pick you up from the airport. You can rent a car from an agency near the airport but you'll see the island a lot better on a bicycle, which you'll probably find at your resort.

PIERCE & NEWMAN

On Little Cayman, a bike is just right for getting around.

Entry

U.S. and Canadian citizens need proof of citizenship—a passport or a birth certificate and photo ID—and a return ticket. Visitors from other countries, including Britain and British dependent territories, must have a passport and return ticket.

Money

The Cayman Islands are expensive—the fixed exchange rate is US$1.25 to the Cayman dollar (CI$). You can use U.S. dollars everywhere but change will be in the local currency. Automatic teller machines are available and major credit cards and traveler's checks are readily accepted on all the islands.

Tipping Your Divemaster

Dive boat crews perform just about every task imaginable, from rescuing panicked divers to hosing off shipboard vomit. You probably know that divemasters and instructors give pre-dive briefings, lead tours and watch out for divers underwater and on board. Do you also know that every year they must take a medic first-aid class? That most of them are qualified to administer oxygen? That they're skilled in the various techniques of rescue, search and recovery? Divemasters are called upon to perform many tasks, from the most mundane, such as loading tanks and passing out cups of water, to the most critical—saving lives.

Most dive operators encourage divers to tip for good service. Particularly in the Caymans, where the cost of living is very high, tips can substantially affect a divemaster's income and quality of life.

Still, tipping can be an awkward practice and divers are frequently left confused. How much is a reasonable tip? And what to do when a dive boat has more than one divemaster, perhaps an instructor, a skipper and sometimes a first mate? Who should be tipped? Each person individually? Just the divemaster?

Most Cayman dive operators recommend a standard tip of 15% of the dive bill. Nevertheless, tipping should not be automatic or considered obligatory. As in a restaurant, the tip should reflect your level of satisfaction. If you aren't happy with the service, tip less or not at all. Conversely, if you feel an extra effort was made, tip extra.

There is little agreement about who should receive the tip. In many cases, tips are distributed equally among the crew, so you should hand your tip to the boat captain or to your divemaster. Other operators feel that crew members should be tipped individually, while still others say that an all-crew tip should be augmented by individual tips for any crew member who takes that extra step to make sure your dive was safe and enjoyable. For teaching dives, instructors should be tipped individually.

If you are diving with a group, be sure to ask about the dive operator's policy before tipping. Many group charters will wait until the end of the charter and tip all at once, while some operators will charge groups of eight or more a standard gratuity as part of the initial dive bill.

Time

The Cayman Islands are on Eastern Standard Time, which is five hours behind GMT. When it's noon in the Cayman Islands, it's 9am in San Francisco, 5pm in London and 3am the following morning in Sydney. Daylight saving time is not observed.

Electricity

The current is 110 volts/60 cycles, as in the U.S. and Canada. Plugs are also U.S.-standard, with two flat parallel prongs. Most lodgings have outlets with a third grounding hole to accommodate computers, chargers, etc. Be sure to bring adapters and converters for equipment that runs on 220 volts.

Weights & Measures

Though speed limits are posted in kilometers per hour, the imperial system is used primarily. Temperature is measured in degrees Fahrenheit, length in yards and feet, and weight in pounds and ounces. This book provides both metric and imperial measurements except for specific references within dive site descriptions, which are given in imperial units. For reference, use the conversion chart inside the back cover of this book.

What to Bring

Bring casual, comfortable attire. For most restaurants, nice resort wear is fine. Remember that the Cayman Islands are a conservative, "proper" British colony—bathing suits and skimpy clothing are inappropriate off the beach and resort areas. A lightweight rain jacket is useful in fall and winter and you'll be happy to have a cover-up on the dive boat to protect from sunburn. On Grand Cayman you can get everything you need, but the selection of goods is more limited on the Sister Islands. In general, you'll save money if you bring your own batteries and film.

Grand Cayman has a couple of excellent shops that sell divers' supplies as well as many full-service dive operators that sell and rent equipment. High-quality dive gear can also be rented from dive shops on the Sister Islands. Tanks used in the Caymans have a 3000psi K-valve, which is U.S.-standard. If you normally use a DIN valve, be sure to bring an adapter. Though the water is warm, it's wise to bring a 2 or 3mm neoprene tropical suit or something comparable. For shore diving you'll want hard-sole booties.

PIERCE & NEWMAN

Underwater photo opportunities, and expert instruction, abound in the Caymans.

Underwater Photography

With so many great topside and underwater photo opportunities, it's lucky that the Caymans also have first-rate photo services. You can rent both still and video cameras on all three islands and E-6 slide processing is widely available. Many Cayman dive operators have excellent photo centers where you can purchase supplies, rent cameras and take underwater photo and video courses. See the Listings section for underwater photography and video services.

Business Hours

Banking hours are Monday through Thursday 9am to 4pm and Friday 9am to 4:30pm. Other businesses are open weekdays 9am to 5pm but most shops stay open later and are also open on weekends. In George Town, however, most shops are closed on Sunday.

Accommodations

The Cayman Islands have more than 2,300 hotel rooms and 2,000 self-catering condominium and villa units featuring one or more bedrooms. Most Grand Cayman accommodations are on the island's West End near Seven Mile Beach and George Town, though there are a few places to stay on the East End as well. Accommodations range from modest dive lodges to five-star resorts. A condo can be a good option for a family. They're usually more spacious and allow you to save money by doing some of your own cooking. Typically, the dive resorts offer lodging and diving packages—after all, this is where the packaged dive trip originated. Most resorts have a dive operator on the premises.

Attractive cottages dot the Cayman countryside.

There are fewer lodging options on the Sister Islands, but you can't go wrong with any of them. Properties on Cayman Brac are found mainly on the south shore of the West End. These include three resorts, which have on-site restaurants and dive operations, as well as a few condos. Lodgings on Little Cayman range from three cozy island hideaways to a "humongous" 40-room resort and a few condos and home rentals. The lodgings in the Sister Islands tend to be casual and friendly and they'll take care of all your diving needs. Many do not have phones or TVs, so if those are important to you, be sure to inquire before making a booking.

For all accommodations, a 10% government room tax and, usually, an automatic 10% gratuity will be added to your bill.

Little Cayman's resorts are concentrated on the island's West End.

Dining & Food

Grand Cayman has more than a hundred restaurants, fast-food outlets and small snack bars, so visitors have a range of options. Most resorts have on-site restaurants, many of which are quite good, offering a variety of local and international dishes. Some resort packages include breakfast, but you'll usually be on your own for lunch and dinner. Independent restaurants are concentrated on the West End but other treasures are scattered about the island—don't be afraid to explore. You'll find everything here from Tex-Mex to Thai. Several supermarkets offer a wide selection, including good wines and gourmet foods.

Cayman Brac has a few small local restaurants and three hotel restaurants, as well as a couple of good markets. On Little Cayman the choice is easy, as there's only one independent restaurant and one well-stocked grocery store. Despite its diminutive size, Little Cayman offers exceptional cuisine at its resorts—some of the clientele comes *solely* for the cuisine. All of the kitchens are excellent, but Pirate's Point and Southern Cross, especially, feature truly gourmet meals. Non-guests are welcome at all the resorts, with advance reservations.

A gratuity might be added to your restaurant bill automatically, so be sure to check before you add on a tip.

Be sure to try some local Cayman fare such as turtle and conch (pronounced *konk*). Farm-raised turtle meat is widely available—any turtle dish you eat in the Caymans is almost guaranteed to be ecologically upright. Marinated conch mixed with onions, peppers and lime juice is a popular dish served on boat excursions. On Little Cayman, you can go conching and taste the bivalve straight from the shell. For vegetables, try callaloo (a leafy green similar to spinach), plantains (a starchy relative of the banana) and ackee, a fruit that tastes and is prepared like a vegetable. The Caribbean's standard fare of rice and red beans (or peas) cooked in coconut milk is popular. Unless you're a vegetarian, be sure to sample the Jamaican-style jerk, where meat is rubbed with spices and slow-smoked over a low fire—it's delicious and popular with locals, so be sure to arrive at the barbecue early. On menus you'll see food that is prepared "Cayman-style," which means with peppers, onions and tomato. Allspice is often added to foods, as is the spicy Scotch bonnet pepper. To wash it all down, try Stingray, the local beer. Desalination plants provide the islands with excellent potable tap water, but bottled water is also available.

PIERCE & NEWMAN

Preparing conch on Little Cayman.

Shopping

The Cayman Islands are duty-free, so you'll find loads of stores in George Town and a few on Cayman Brac selling brand-name jewelry, perfume, china, crystal and designer labels from all over the world. Shops are also found along Grand Cayman's West Bay Road and in the resorts. Just north of the Grand Cayman Ferry Terminal is the Glassblowing Studio (☎ 949-8312), where you can watch molten glass take shape and purchase handmade glassware. For arts and crafts from the Caymans and around the Caribbean, visit Pure Art Gallery & Gifts (☎ 949-9133) on South Church Street and the Cayman Islands National Museum's gift shop (☎ 949-8368) in George Town. Both carry a nice selection of hand-crafted items—baskets, purses, brooms, hats, etc.—made from the local silver thatch palm, the official tree of the Caymans.

If you're visiting the Brac, check out the caymanite, a semiprecious stone found in the island's limestone bluff. In Stake Bay (look for several windmills in the front yard) you'll find Eddie Scott, a fascinating and inventive man who crafts jewelry made from the stone. It's also available at NIM (Native Island Made) Things on the East End. On Little Cayman, visit sweet little Mrs. Reilly who weaves lovely baskets—a double treat.

You'll see turtle-shell items for sale in the Caymans. Most of these items are made from farm-raised turtles rather than from endangered wild turtles. Still, you should be aware that your home country may prohibit the importation of turtle-shell products of any kind, whether farm-raised or not.

PIERCE & NEWMAN

Watch artisans at work in George Town's Glassblowing Studio.

MICHAEL LAWRENCE

Cayman Brac's large limestone bluff is riddled with caves that visitors can explore.

Activities & Attractions

For nondivers, as well as anyone who needs to release a little nitrogen, Grand Cayman has plenty of out-of-water activities and attractions. Activities on the Sister Islands tend to be more limited, so if lots of topside action is important to you, Grand Cayman is probably the better choice.

PIERCE & NEWMAN

Grand Cayman

Boat Excursions

Catamaran cruises are a fun and relaxing way to experience the islands. Choose from sunset sails, dinner cruises and, of course, Stingray City snorkel sails. Parrot's Landing operates the *Cockatoo*, a beautiful 60ft racing catamaran. Red Sail Sports has two luxury catamarans—the 62ft *Spirit of Cayman* and the 65ft *Spirit of Ppalu*. The *Nancy* (☎ 949-8988) is a tall ship, while the *Jolly Roger* (☎ 949-8534) is a pirate ship replica that kids will enjoy.

Blowholes

Look for signs directing you to the blowhole areas along the southern coastal road just before you reach the East End. It's fun to see the explosion of water blast up through holes in the ironshore, but the main reason to visit is for the scenic drive and panoramic vistas on the long southern coastline.

Cayman Turtle Farm

Thousands of green sea turtles (endangered in the wild) are bred and raised in pools at the Cayman Turtle Farm (☎ 949-3894) on West Bay Road, north of Seven Mile Beach. You'll see turtles ranging in size from tiny hatchlings to adults weighing as much as 600lbs (270kg). Though many of the turtles are released into the wild, most are bred for consumption both here and abroad. Feeding time is usually between 3:15 and 3:30pm—an

PIERCE & NEWMAN

Hatchlings swim in tanks at the world's only commercial sea turtle farm.

excellent time to check out the turtles in action. You'll also see indigenous flora and fauna including the Cayman green parrot, iguanas and crocodiles. Though some may find it a macabre way to keep with the theme, the snack bar features turtle soup, turtle sandwiches and other light meals. This is one of the few places in the world that you can eat turtle and be assured that you aren't contributing to the decimation of a species. The gift shop carries a wide selection of souvenirs, especially of the turtle-oriented variety. Remember, your home country may have conservation laws prohibiting the importation of items made from turtle shell.

Historic Sites

An excursion to the **Pedro St. James National Historic Site** (☎ 947-3329) in Savannah is a terrific way to spend a couple of hours. Tour the beautifully restored 19th-century West Indian Great House, which has lovely ocean views. You can also stroll around the 8-acre (3-hectare) estate, complete with cannons facing out to sea. This was the home of William Eden, a mariner and early English settler who established a cotton and mahogany plantation on Savannah's Pedro Bluff. The site's main historic importance dates to 1831, when residents met here to decide to elect their first legislative assembly.

PIERCE & NEWMAN

Experience 19th-century island life at Pedro St. James historic site.

Construction details—such as rough-hewn timber beams and wooden pegs—reflect authentic building techniques of early 19th-century Caribbean great houses. A working bake oven and outdoor kitchen are re-creations of outbuildings on the original estate. The beautiful gardens are planted with fruit trees, tropical plants, vegetables and medicinal plants representative of a small West Indian plantation. The site is open daily 8:30am to 5pm.

The attractive restored 19th-century building facing George Town Harbour is home to the **Cayman Islands National Museum** (☎ 949-8368). It originally housed government offices and the town jail. Today it features art, artifacts and fun interactive exhibits designed to preserve the Cayman heritage. The cultural history exhibit shows how islanders survived in the early days when they had little contact with the rest of the world. Divers will enjoy the natural history exhibit's three-dimensional map showing the dramatic panorama of undersea mountains and canyons that surround the islands. Also, a laser-disc presentation offers a porthole view to the underwater world. The museum is open weekdays 9am to 5pm and Saturday 10am to 2pm.

Another particularly enjoyable way to learn about local history and architecture is to take a **self-guided walking tour**. The National Trust publishes excellent booklets for West Bay, George Town and Bodden Town—pick one up at any of the historic sites.

Nature Excursions

See and learn about Cayman's beautiful native flora and fauna while getting some healthy exercise at the 65-acre (26-hectare) **Queen Elizabeth II Botanic Park** (☎ 947-9462). The park features a nature trail almost a mile (1.6km) in length as well as colorful gardens, 10 acres (4 hectares) of wetlands and an old Cayman home with traditional gardens. Relax in the outdoor café or teahouse. A scenic 30-minute drive along the southern coastal highway from George Town brings you to the park. It's open daily 9am to 6:30pm, with the last entrance at 5:30.

Hike the **Mastic Trail**, which served as a shortcut to the North Side in the late 1800s. The 2½-hour guided tour from Frank Sound will put you in touch with Cayman vegetation and wildlife. Call Silver Thatch Excursions (☎ 949-1996) for information and reservations.

Cardinal D's Park, just outside of George Town, is the place to see exotic birds. The park features more than 60 species of birds, as well as miniature ponies.

Rum Point

Try to end a day of island touring at Rum Point on the island's North Side. This park-like beach area is a great spot to relax, enjoy a refreshing mudslide (a sweet and potent mixture of vodka and coffee and Irish cream liqueurs) from the bar and watch for the green flash at sunset. If you come during the day, you can grab a lunch and enjoy a variety of watersports. Alternately, Red Sail Sports runs the 120-passenger *Rum Pointer* ferry across the North Sound. This scenic half-hour cruise departs from the Hyatt Canal.

PIERCE & MORRISEY

A spectacular sunset ends the day at Rum Point.

Snorkeling Charters

Bayside Watersports runs two-hour and half-day excursions to a variety of choice snorkeling sites around the island, including the southeast barrier reef, Aquarium and Sandbar (the secondary stingray-feeding site). Transportation to and from your lodging is provided, as is lunch. Check schedules and make reservations at Bayside's offices at Morgan's Harbour Marina (☎ 949-3200) and in The Falls Shopping Center (☎ 949-1750).

Chartered snorkeling trips can bring you to great shallow sites like the *Geneva Kathleen* wreck.

Submarines & Semi-Submersibles

You don't have to be a diver to see the colorful underwater world of the Cayman Islands. Corals, sponges, fish and other marine life are on view from the large portholes of the 48-passenger submarine *Atlantis XI.* The vessel dives to 100ft (30m) daily (except Sunday) on the West Wall, south of George Town. That's deep, but it's not as impressive as a trip on the Research Submersible, which can take you and a single other passenger 800ft (240m) below the surface. Both subs are air-conditioned and pressurized for your comfort. For information, call Atlantis Submarines (☎ 949-7700).

Two semi-submersibles—the 34-passenger *SeaWorld Explorer* (☎ 949-8534) and the 60-passenger *Nautilus* (☎ 945-1355)—cruise along at just 5ft (1.5m) below the water's surface, accompanied by excellent narrated tours describing the local marine habitats. All of the subs and semi-submersibles are berthed in George Town Harbour.

Watersports

Most Grand Cayman resorts have watersports centers that can arrange parasailing, ocean kayaking, sailing or other activities. Check at resorts along Seven Mile Beach, at Morritt's Tortuga Club on the East End and at Rum Point on the North Side.

The reef-protected shallows of the windy East End are Grand Cayman's primo locale for **windsurfing**. Rent boards from BIC Windsurfing Center at Morritt's Tortuga Club. On Seven Mile Beach, the Mistral Windsurfing Center next to Plantana Condominiums offers rentals and instruction.

Cayman Brac

Caves

Nature carved a network of caves into Cayman Brac's limestone bluffs. Over the years, these caves have provided island inhabitants with shelter during storms. In fact, when most of the homes on the islands were destroyed during a devastating 1932 hurricane, the caves saved many lives. Look for signs along the road pointing out caves that are appropriate for exploration by visitors. Though most of the caves are large and open with interesting stalactite and stalagmite formations, you may want to bring a flashlight for exploring the recesses. In general, the caves are very safe—no special knowledge of spelunking is needed to explore them.

PIERCE & MORRISEY

Cayman Brac's enormous caves provide shelter for islanders.

Look for **Peter's Cave** high up on the bluff. It can be accessed either from Spot Bay or from a side road off the road to the lighthouse. Steps and handrails lead up to the entrance, but you'll have to duck down and almost crawl before entering the open chamber. **Rebecca's Cave**, on the south shore near the West End, was named after a young girl who died there. Along the south shore road, **Bat Cave** is accessed by a ladder and has long trailing vines. And, yes, there are bats inside. **Great Cave**, on the south shore of the East End, has beautiful rock formations. To get to it you'll have to climb up a series of ladders. Wooden steps lead into the entrance of **Skull Cave**, which looks like a skull. Skull Cave is near the hospital on the north shore.

Cayman Brac Museum

Go "Brac" in time to learn what island life was like in the old days at the Cayman Brac Museum (☎ 948-2622) in the old government administration building in Stake Bay. Most displays and exhibits highlight the shipbuilding era of the early 20th century when the Brac was still fairly isolated from the outside world. The museum is open weekdays 9am to noon and 1 to 4pm and Saturday 9am to noon.

Hiking & Bird-Watching

Hike the nature trails on the East End bluff and find century plants, bright yellow shamrock and glorious views. If you think you see some moving pebbles, take a closer look—these are actually soldier crabs scurrying about with their little homes on their backs. One of the trails cuts through the 180-acre (72-hectare) **Brac Parrot Reserve**. In addition to the endangered Brac parrot, you can see frigate birds, brown boobies and many other bird species.

Little Cayman

Booby Pond Nature Reserve

Protected by the National Trust, this 204-acre (82-hectare) salt-water lagoon is the breeding area for the rare red-footed booby and the magnificent frigate bird. The reserve is also a major stopover for dozens of species of migrating shorebirds, so depending on the time of year you visit, you might see herons, egrets or black-necked stilts, among others.

The Visitors Center will tell you all about the flora and fauna in the reserve and give you an opportunity to watch the birds through one of the two high-powered telescopes. The reserve is just north of Blossom Village.

MICHAEL LAWRENCE

An egret rests on Booby Pond.

Owen Island

This scenic 11-acre (4-hectare) island is just 200 yards (180m) offshore and is part of the South Sound reef. Ringed completely by a sandy beach, it's perfect for snorkeling, bonefishing, conching and picnicking.

Fishing

Bonefish, small tarpon and permit make for exciting angling in the knee-deep shallows. It's mostly catch-and-release around here, but conching is also a lot of fun and could make dinnertime a treat. Contact Sam McCoy's Diving & Fishing Lodge or Southern Cross Club to arrange for a guide and equipment.

MICHAEL LAWRENCE

Popular with anglers, Little Cayman's Tarpon Lake is home to an unusual population of tarpon. The fish are much smaller than the tarpon you'll see when diving.

Diving Health & Safety

PIERCE & NEWMAN

General Health

A generally healthy destination, the Cayman Islands do not require innoculations unless you are arriving from a high-risk area, such as tropical South America. The main danger to visitors is usually the sun—use plenty of sunscreen or cover up well to prevent sunburn, and be sure to drink plenty of water to prevent dehydration.

The U.S. Centers for Disease Control & Prevention regularly posts updates on health-related concerns around the world specifically for travelers. Contact the CDC by fax or visit their website. Call (toll-free from the U.S.) ☎ 888-232-3299 and request Document 000005 to receive a list of documents available by fax. The website is www.cdc.gov.

Pre-Trip Preparation

Your general state of health, diving skill level and specific equipment needs are the three most important factors that impact any dive trip. If you honestly assess these before you leave, you'll be well on your way to assuring a safe dive trip.

First, if you're not in shape, start exercising. Second, if you haven't dived for a while (six months is too long) and your skills are rusty, do a local dive with an experienced buddy or take a scuba review course. Finally, inspect your dive gear. Feeling good physically, diving with experience and with reliable equipment will not only increase your safety, but will also enhance your enjoyment underwater.

At least a month before your trip, inspect your dive gear. Remember, your regulator should be serviced annually, whether you've used it or not. If you use a dive computer and can replace the battery yourself, change it before the trip or buy a spare one to take along. Otherwise, send the computer to the manufacturer for a battery replacement.

If possible, find out if the dive center rents or services the type of gear you own. If not, you might want to take spare parts or even spare gear. A spare mask is always a good idea.

Purchase any additional equipment you might need, such as a dive light and

Diving & Flying

Many divers in the Cayman Islands arrive by plane. While it's fine to dive soon *after* flying, it's important to remember that your last dive should be completed at least 12 hours (some experts advise 24 hours, particularly after repetitive dives) *before* your flight to minimize the risk of decompression sickness, caused by residual nitrogen in the blood.

tank marker light for night diving, a line reel for wreck diving, etc. Make sure you have at least a whistle attached to your BC. Better yet, add a marker tube (also known as a safety sausage or come-to-me).

About a week before taking off, do a final check of your gear, grease o-rings, check batteries and assemble a save-a-dive kit. This kit should at minimum contain extra mask and fin straps, snorkel keeper, mouthpiece, valve cap, zip ties and o-rings. Don't forget to pack a first-aid kit and medications such as decongestants, ear drops, antihistamines and seasickness tablets.

Stay clear of divers getting onto the boat, particularly in rough water.

Tips for Evaluating a Dive Operator

First impressions mean a lot. Does the business appear organized and professionally staffed? Does it prominently display a dive affiliation such as NAUI, PADI, SSI, etc.? These are both good indications that it adheres to high standards.

When you come to dive, a well-run business will always have paperwork for you to fill out. At the least, someone should look at your certification card and ask when you last dived. If they want to see your logbook or check basic skills in the water, even better.

Rental equipment should be well rinsed. If you see sand or salt crystals, watch out, as their presence could indicate sloppy equipment care. Before starting your dive, inspect the equipment thoroughly: Check hoses for wear, see that mouthpieces are secure and make sure they've given you a depth gauge and air pressure gauge.

After you gear up and turn on your air, listen for air leaks. Now test your BC: Push the power inflator to make sure it functions correctly and doesn't free-flow; if it fails, get another BC—don't try to inflate it manually; make sure the BC holds air. Then purge your regulator a bit and smell the air. It should be odorless. If you detect an oily or otherwise bad smell, try a different tank, then start searching for another operator.

Tips for Evaluating a Dive Boat

Before departure, take a good look at the craft you will be diving from. A well-outfitted dive boat has communication with on-shore services. It also carries oxygen, a recall device and a first-aid kit. A well-prepared crew will give a thorough pre-dive briefing that explains procedures for dealing with an emergency when divers are in the water. The briefing also explains how divers should enter the water and get back on board. A larger boat should have a shaded area and a supply of fresh drinking water.

If there is a strong current, the crew might provide a special descent line and should be able to throw out a drift line from the stern. For deep dives, the crew should hang a safety tank at 15ft (5m). On night dives, a good boat will have powerful lights, including a strobe light.

When carrying groups, a good crew will get everyone's name on the dive roster so that it can initiate an immediate search if a diver is missing. This is something you should always verify.

DAN

Divers Alert Network (DAN) is an international membership association of individuals and organizations sharing a common interest in diving and safety. It operates a 24-hour diving emergency hotline in the U.S.: ☎ **919-684-8111 or 919-684-4DAN** (-4326). The latter accepts collect calls in a dive emergency. Though DAN does not directly provide medical care, it does provide advice on early treatment, evacuation and hyperbaric treatment of diving-related injuries. Divers should contact DAN for assistance as soon as a diving emergency is suspected.

DAN membership is reasonably priced and includes DAN TravelAssist, a membership benefit that covers medical air evacuation from anywhere in the world for any illness or injury. For a small additional fee, divers can get secondary insurance coverage for decompression illness. For membership questions, contact DAN at ☎ 800-446-2671 in the U.S. or ☎ 919-684-2948 elsewhere. DAN can also be reached at www.diversalertnetwork.org.

Medical & Recompression Facilities

Grand Cayman's **George Town Hospital** (☎ 949-8600 or 911 in an emergency) is a modern facility with an emergency room and 24-hour ambulance paramedic service. The hospital operates a two-person double-lock recompression chamber, which is staffed around the clock and supervised by a physician experienced in hyperbaric medicine.

On Cayman Brac, **Faith Hospital** (☎ 948-2242) is at Stake Bay. For medical care on Little Cayman, a **clinic** (☎ 948-1051) near the airport is staffed by a nurse.

Wreck Diving & Deep Diving

The Cayman Islands offer a vast array of diving environments from easy shallow dives to more complex deep dives and wreck dives. For your safety, it is important that you understand some of the dangers associated with certain types of diving.

- **Wreck Diving** If done properly, wreck diving can be safe and fascinating. Penetration of shipwrecks, however, is a skilled specialty and should not be attempted without proper training. Wrecks are often unstable; they can be silty, deep and disorienting. Use an experienced guide to view any challenging wrecks and the amazing coral communities that have developed on them.

- **Deep Diving** Opportunities to dive deep abound in the Cayman Islands. Many attractions are beyond 130ft (40m), the recognized maximum depth limit of sport diving. Before venturing beyond these limits, it is imperative that divers be specially trained in deep diving and/or technical diving. Classes will teach you to recognize symptoms of nitrogen narcosis and proper decompression procedures when doing deep or repetitive deep dives. Know your limits and don't push your luck when it comes to depth.

PIERCE & NEWMAN

The *Tibbetts* is the only diveable Russian-built warship in the Western Hemisphere.

Diving in the Cayman Islands

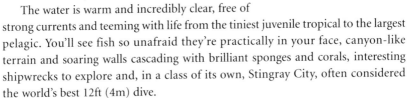

Consider diving and snorkeling anywhere in the Cayman Islands to be nothing less than a privilege. These three islands alone could keep any bubble-blower happy for a lifetime. Fringing reefs, shallow shelves and quick shoreline drop-offs give snorkelers and divers almost instant access to both shallow and deep reef environments.

PIERCE & NEWMAN

The water is warm and incredibly clear, free of strong currents and teeming with life from the tiniest juvenile tropical to the largest pelagic. You'll see fish so unafraid they're practically in your face, canyon-like terrain and soaring walls cascading with brilliant sponges and corals, interesting shipwrecks to explore and, in a class of its own, Stingray City, often considered the world's best 12ft (4m) dive.

Nearly all dive businesses in the Cayman Islands have full-service operations with equipment sales and rentals, on-site air compressors and courses from introduction to scuba through rescue or divemaster. Nitrox instruction is particularly in demand here and EANx32 is used widely. If shops don't pump it on-site, they can usually obtain fills for customers and their divemasters.

The 56 dive sites profiled in this book are broken down into three regions: Grand Cayman (which is further separated into Northern, West End and East End sites), Cayman Brac and Little Cayman. These sites represent some of the top dive

The Name Game

Though names used for dive sites are fairly standardized in the Caymans, you'll undoubtedly hear some variations. Grand Cayman's Princess Penny's Pinnacle (as we call it) is a good example—you may hear it called Princess Penny's Wall or just Princess Penny's. Fortunately, most variations are similar enough not to cause confusion.

Sites are usually named for a distinguishing physical aspect, either underwater or topside. For instance, practically every island has a site in view of the local runway called Wind Sock. Underwater topography—Patch Reef, Big Tunnel, Round Rock—is an especially common naming device. Another is using the name of an individual (usually deceased)—a site will sometimes have an inscribed plaque at the mooring line to honor the individual. It's always interesting to ask how sites were named because you'll sometimes hear wildly divergent stories. In this guide, we've used the names standardized by the Department of the Environment. Where two completely different names are used for the same site, we've put the less standard name in parentheses.

possibilities of the area's massive underwater reef structures. Altogether, the Department of the Environment maintains some 265 public mooring sites throughout the islands and new sites are added regularly. If you happen to be diving a site that's not described in this guidebook, don't despair—you might be in for a wonderful surprise.

Certification

This is certainly one of the best places in the world to get certified or to do your Open Water dives. What could be better? The water is warm and exceptionally clear with beautiful shallow sites, experienced instructors and rigorous safety standards.

All international certifying agencies are represented—which agencies a dive operator uses depends mainly on the training of the particular instructors working there. Dive operators here offer a tremendous number of scuba review and Discover Scuba ("resort") courses, which are appropriate for divers who want to

EANx32: The Nitrox Solution

Enriched air nitrox (EANx) is used widely throughout the Caymans and, although it's a little more expensive than regular breathing air, it is easy to get.

The mixture used in the Caymans is almost exclusively EANx32, which means it's 32% oxygen. Since normal breathing air is 21% oxygen, you'll be getting less nitrogen and more oxygen into your system. Nitrox can increase bottom times, but most divers in the Caymans use it for the extra safety margin and because they say it makes them feel better. Certainly, with less nitrogen and increased oxygen in your system, you'll decrease the risk of decompression sickness.

If you're nitrox certified, be sure to bring your certification card. If you're not certified, you can take one of the many nitrox classes offered by dive operators throughout the islands.

PIERCE & NEWMAN

brush up on their skills or who want a quick dive experience without actually getting certified. Several operators also offer learn-to-snorkel boat trips, which combine instruction, equipment, lunch and snorkeling stops.

If you're planning to do your Open Water checkout dives for certification, remember to get a referral from your classroom instructor.

Dive Site Icons

The symbols at the beginning of the dive site descriptions provide a quick summary of some of the important characteristics of each site:

 Good snorkeling or free-diving site.

 Remains or partial remains of a wreck can be seen at this site.

 Sheer wall or drop-off.

 Deep dive. Features of this dive occur in water deeper than 90ft (27m).

 Strong currents may be encountered at this site.

 Strong surge (the horizontal movement of water caused by waves) may be encountered at this site.

 Shore dive. This site can be accessed from shore.

 Caves or caverns are prominent features of this site. Only experienced cave divers should explore inner cave areas.

 Marine preserve. Special protective regulations apply in this area.

Pisces Rating System for Dives & Divers

The dive sites in this book are rated according to the following system. These are not absolute ratings but apply to divers at a particular time, diving at a particular place. For instance, someone unfamiliar with prevailing conditions might be considered a novice diver at one dive area, but an intermediate diver at another, more familiar location.

Novice: A novice diver should be accompanied by an instructor, divemaster or advanced diver on all dives. A novice diver generally fits the following profile:

◆ basic scuba certification from an internationally recognized certifying agency
◆ dives infrequently (less than one trip a year)
◆ logged fewer than 25 total dives
◆ little or no experience diving in similar waters and conditions
◆ dives no deeper than 60ft (18m)

Intermediate: An intermediate diver generally fits the following profile:

◆ may have participated in some form of continuing diver education
◆ logged between 25 and 100 dives
◆ dives no deeper than 130ft (40m)
◆ has been diving in similar waters and conditions within the last six months

Advanced: An advanced diver generally fits the following profile:

◆ advanced certification
◆ has been diving for more than two years and logged over 100 dives
◆ has been diving in similar waters and conditions within the last six months

Regardless of your skill level, you should be in good physical condition and know your limitations. If you are uncertain of your own level of expertise for a particular site, ask the advice of a local dive instructor. He or she is best qualified to assess your abilities based on the site's prevailing dive conditions. Ultimately, however, you must decide if you are capable of making a particular dive, a decision that should take into account your level of training, recent experience and physical condition, as well as the conditions at the site. Remember that conditions can change at any time, even during a dive.

Grand Cayman Dive Sites

Grand Cayman is flat and scenic with wonderful coastline vistas. The shoreline has some sandy stretches, but it's primarily rough rock-like ironshore. Though dive sites surround the island and all have easy access, diving activity is centered mainly on the West End, where weather conditions are stable and lodgings and dive operators are nearby. A small fraction of visiting divers venture to the East End, where they are well rewarded for their efforts.

You'll encounter both sloping and precipitous walls cracked with tunnels and swim-throughs and cascading with multicolored sponges and corals. You'll also find shallow reefs teeming with tiny invertebrates, schooling fish and solitary tropicals. Coral-encrusted shipwrecks add to the area's interest. In a class of its own is Stingray City, the famed shallow area favored by dozens of friendly stingrays.

Grand Cayman is an excellent destination for both divers and snorkelers. With a selection of 154 moored sites, a nondiving day is almost unheard of, regardless of the weather. Unless conditions are extremely stormy, operators can always find a lee—an area sheltered from the wind. This section covers 32 of Grand Cayman's best dive sites, separated into Northern, West End and East End sites.

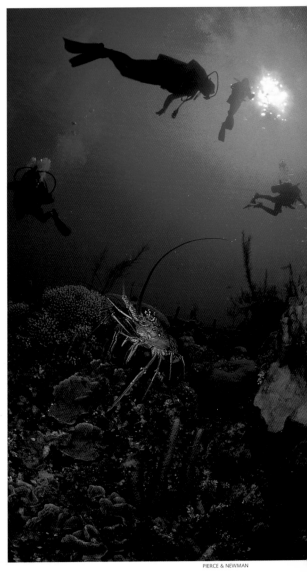

PIERCE & NEWMAN

Even lobsters feel safe in Cayman's protected areas.

45

Shore Diving & Snorkeling on Grand Cayman

Don't be disappointed if you can't get out on a boat—the shore diving on Grand Cayman can keep you happy for weeks *and* it'll save you a lot of money. Shore-diving sites are excellent for snorkelers as well. Several West End shore-diving facilities—including Eden Rock Diving Centre, Parrot's Landing, Sunset Divers and

Quabo Dives—rent weights and tanks and have easy access to superb reefs. For diving on the northwest shore, visit Turtle Reef Divers, just north of the Cayman Turtle Farm. To the far north is, of course, Stingray City, but there's also shore diving from Rum Point, which is a good place to find conch. On the West End is the wreck of the *Cali* in George Town Harbour. On the south side, look for Pedro's Castle.

Northern Dive Sites

Two striking geographic features dominate the northwest coast. One is the North Sound, an enormous shallow lagoon that extends from Conch Point on the west to Rum Point on the east. Separating the sound from the sea is a fringing reef that comes right up to the surface, so boat access to the sound is restricted to just three channels. The very shallow sound is home to Stingray City, one of the world's most popular dive and snorkel sites.

Grand Cayman Northern Dive Sites	Good Snorkeling	Novice	Intermediate	Advanced
1 White Stroke Canyon			●	
2 Robert's Wall			●	
3 Leslie's Curl			●	
4 Eagle Ray Pass			●	
5 Princess Penny's Pinnacle			●	
6 Stingray City	●	●		

Just outside the sound is another equally impressive feature—the North Wall. It crests at about 40 to 60ft (12 to 18m) and runs parallel to the coast, virtually in a straight line. Because the north shore is often windy and seas are rough, divers exploring the north coast sites must have sufficient experience. Boats are often restricted altogether. Nevertheless, this is an exciting diving area where you'll spot lots of pelagic life.

Surf pounds the rough coastline on the north shore.

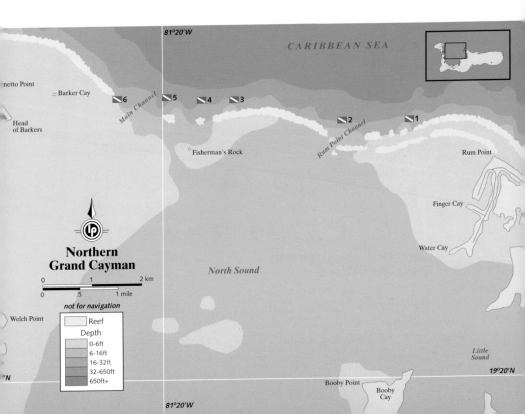

1 White Stroke Canyon

Few dive boats travel this far east on the north coast. Water conditions are usually choppy, so divers who make the trip should be accustomed to surging seas. Beneath the waves, you'll find a real treat—an enormous craggy canyon where every inch is covered with vibrant

Location: North Wall

Depth Range: 60-100ft (18-30m)

Access: Boat

Expertise Rating: Intermediate

A bold lobster observes strange intruders.

life forms, and a wall that plunges to depths your gauges should never register.

At 60ft, you'll reach the top of a reef, which hosts turtles and fluttering French angelfish. Eels hunker back into the coral crevices and occasionally a lobster will appear in daylight, boldly strutting its stuff. As you descend the wall, you'll enter canyon-like terrain with gorge-cut walls. At 100ft look down over the wall into the blue abyss and watch for sharks, eagle rays and other visitors from the deep. Lacy sea fans, sponges and black coral communities decorate this section of the healthy North Wall. As you head back to the boat, watch for eagle rays that might be feeding in the sand near the mooring line.

2 Robert's Wall

This dramatic section of the North Wall features large cuts with over-hanging coral structures and deep swim-throughs. Along the wall you'll swim by large barrel sponges, swaying anemones and black coral in profusion. Off the edge of the wall you'll typically see spotted eagle rays and turtles visiting from the vast bottomless blue beyond. Off the wall in blue water, black-tipped reef sharks and hammerheads are frequent visitors.

Location: North Wall

Depth Range: 50-100ft (15-30m)

Access: Boat

Expertise Rating: Intermediate

Although it's tempting, don't stay too long and be sure to watch that depth gauge. As you gradually make your way back up to the top of the reef, look for olive-colored filefish, either solitary or in pairs, finding shelter among gorgonians. Lobsters and crabs typically congregate on the edge of the wall, while green moray eels stay near the sandbar. For this deep site, divemasters recommend a standard safety stop at 15ft.

A green sea turtle observes the reef life near the wall.

3   Leslie's Curl

At this site, as with much of the wall north of the main channel and along most of the north shore, the top of the wall is deep. Bottom times are frustratingly short and you should take care to monitor your depth. As you descend this slice of wall, you'll find nice cuts and crevices between about 78 and 83ft.

While hugging the wall, occasionally peer into the deep waters for pelagics,

Location: North Wall

Depth Range: 60-100ft (18-30m)

Access: Boat

Expertise Rating: Intermediate

those elusive denizens of the deep. They sometimes come in to check out the reef life along the north shore. Along the wall, purple sea fans and sea whips protrude, reaching up toward the light. Look for large anemones with white tentacles and lavender tips— occasionally you'll find a little crab or shrimp nestled among them. In the shallows, juvenile turtles crane their long necks toward the sun—they look like they could be sunbathing.

Giant anemones can reach up to a foot wide.

EAGLE VALLEY LIBRARY DISTRICT
P.O. BOX 240   600 BROADWAY
EAGLE, CO 81631   (970) 328-8800

4 Eagle Ray Pass

If you don't spy a spotted eagle ray soaring through the pass here, you'll probably see these graceful creatures patrolling along the wall or hunting for food in the sandy shallows. This section of the North Wall is just west of Leslie's Curl and in the middle of the main channel, where pelagic life is abundant.

As you descend the mooring line, look for both the sandy "pass" through this canyon-like terrain and the large sandy chute that flows between steep walls of coral. Forming a funnel-like V shape, the passage narrows as you swim through it. The buttresses of coral almost converge overhead. Follow the chute at a depth of about 70ft and it will deposit you right out over the wall, where you can continue your descent.

Healthy sponges, anemones and plate corals accent the face of the wall. Look for the eagle rays. Turtles are also common visitors—usually the hawksbill. Check out the nooks and crannies of the wall. You're likely to spot lobsters and eels, while the occasional queen angelfish will keep a safe distance. If there's time, you might want to explore the smaller canyons flanking the chute.

Location: North Wall

Depth Range: 52-100ft (16-30m)

Access: Boat

Expertise Rating: Intermediate

PIERCE & MORRISEY

A queen angelfish takes refuge.

PIERCE & NEWMAN

Follow the passage right over the wall.

5 Princess Penny's Pinnacle

Way out in the North Sound where few dive boats venture, Princess Penny's features a single large beautiful pinnacle near the mooring, as well as a couple of narrow swim-throughs that exit down the face of the wall.

Location: North Wall

Depth Range: 45-100ft (14-30m)

Access: Boat

Expertise Rating: Intermediate

From the mooring, head out toward the wall. You'll see the large pinnacle covered with deep-water gorgonians and usually surrounded by a bustling profusion of marine life. Juvenile reef fish swarm around the pinnacle and along the top of the wall. Joining them are large triggerfish, angelfish and yellowtail snapper. You can't miss the large basket sponges that decorate the coral outcroppings.

To reach the face of the wall, swim through the narrow passageway just west of the mooring. It angles downward through the coral, depositing you smack on the wall at about 75ft. Here you'll find layers of plate coral stair-stepping down the precipice and colorful tube, rope and branching sponges protruding into the blue plankton-rich currents. Off of the wall, you are likely to spot hawksbill turtles and spotted eagle rays, which occasionally cruise in from the deep. You'll find another swim-through on the wall at about 90ft, just east of this one. Traverse

Deep-water gorgonians decorate Princess Penny's Pinnacle.

your way through this steep coral passage and you'll find yourself back on top of the wall, at about 45ft.

6 Stingray City

This effortless marine encounter with friendly (and hungry) stingrays is truly an amazing experience. The stingray feedings take place both here and at a nearby site called **Sandbar**, which is a bit shallower. Your divemaster will provide a small container of squid for each diver to take down. Simply jump off the boat and drop to your knees on the sandy seafloor (if you're diving) or hover on the surface (if you're snorkeling). Whatever you do, hug that container of squid to your body!

Gentle southern stingrays will immediately glide over to check out the menu. Don't be surprised at your popularity—it's not unusual to have three or more rays begging for your attention. With vacuum-cleaner efficiency, they'll attempt to suck up the little squid morsels grasped in your hand. Here you can break all the rules—go ahead and feel the rays' velvety smooth bellies and gently rub their heads just between the eyes. Amazingly, they really do seem to enjoy it. Despite those menacing-looking barbs on their tails,

Location: North Sound

Depth Range: 12ft (4m)

Access: Boat

Expertise Rating: Novice

they're very gentle. In fact, they just might completely envelop you—some grow up to 4ft in width—or decide to rest for a bit on top of your head!

A bit of advice: Hold the squid in your hand, making a fist, and don't worry too much about feeding the rays—they get plenty to eat—but watch out for those pesky yellowtail snappers. They're after the same meal and, as their name suggests, they can nip! To avoid losing some skin, make sure no little squid pieces hang out of your hand.

Gloves are not allowed at either stingray-feeding site. Divers should wear a little extra weight and stay kneeling to avoid stirring up the sand.

Stingrays in the Caymans

PIERCE & NEWMAN

If for some reason you can't get to Stingray City, don't despair. Southern stingrays are common to the Caymans, so you're likely to see them at other sites. You shouldn't feed them and you won't be able to feel their soft undersides, but if you approach cautiously while they're snuggled in the sand, you'll be able to get a close look. You can even see them hunt for food—watch as they suck up crustaceans buried in the sand. Often you'll see a bar jack hovering just overhead, hunting right along with the ray. Look for the rays' outlines in the sand—frequently they lie motionless, almost completely buried, with only their eyes peering out.

PIERCE & NEWMAN

With squid in hand, you'll get lots of attention at Stingray City.

West End Dive Sites

Most of Grand Cayman's diving takes place on the West End. Conditions couldn't be better—nice calm water, very little current, excellent visibility and sites just minutes from shore. Though the area's vibrant shallow reefs are ideal for new divers and for those getting reacquainted with the sport, they will enthrall everyone—including those who have already filled a couple of logbooks. Underwater photographers, especially, will be thrilled by the clear water and approachable marine life. Along the entire west coast, marine park protections prohibit fishing, spearing and collecting, so fish tend to be unafraid and brazenly "in your face."

The reef features finger-like coral formations ("spurs"), which extend perpendicular to shore and run parallel to one another out to the West Wall. Coral

Grand Cayman West End Dive Sites	Good Snorkeling	Novice	Intermediate	Advanced
7 Orange Canyon			●	
8 Big Tunnel			●	
9 Little Tunnels			●	
10 Round Rock			●	
11 Trinity Caves			●	
12 Silver Sands		●		
13 Aquarium		●		
14 Governor's (Peter's) Reef		●		
15 Oro Verde		●		
16 Hammerhead Hole		●		
17 Rhapsody (Mesa)		●		
18 Royal Palms Ledge		●		
19 Balboa & Cheeseburger Reef	●	●		
20 Eden Rock & Devil's Grotto	●	●		
21 Parrot's Reef	●	●		
22 Eagle Ray Rock			●	
23 Japanese Gardens			●	

West End
Grand Cayman

not for navigation

Reef
Depth
- 0-6ft
- 6-16ft
- 16-32ft
- 32-650ft
- 650ft+

CARIBBEAN SEA

GEORGE TOWN

North Sound

South Sound

West Bay

Seven Mile Beach

81°25'W

81°20'W

19°20'N

mounds are in very shallow water—generally about 35ft (11m). Narrow sandy grooves run between the spurs like alleyways. These shallow sites are excellent areas for observing small creatures such as banded coral shrimp and arrow crabs. The West Wall crests at about 50ft (15m) and descends in a gradual slope—perfect for intermediate divers.

Like the northwest, the southwest has a sheltering lagoon, so this is where dive operators point their bows when winter storms arise. The South Wall, like the West Wall, slopes gradually, but it starts deeper—about 70 to 85ft (21 to 25m)—and plunges to 6,000ft (1,800m).

Welcome to Hell

The jagged black rock formations in Grand Cayman's northwest once inspired a local official to exclaim, "This is what Hell must look like!" The resulting community name has been a bonanza for the local post office, now painted fire-engine red and employing a resident "devil." This rather benevolent Satan (actually a devout Christian) asks "How the hell are you?" and "Where the hell are you from?" as he dispenses souvenirs.

7 Orange Canyon

As the name suggests, this is canyon-like territory on a steep extension of the North Wall off North West Point. Because it's a deep dive, Orange Canyon is not appropriate for beginners.

The sloping wall is covered with large orange elephant ear sponges and huge

Location: South of North West Point

Depth Range: 61-100ft (18-30m)

Access: Boat

Expertise Rating: Intermediate

STEVE ROSENBERG
Elephant ear sponges lend this site its name.

lavender sea fans. Keep an eye out for stationary frogfish camouflaged on the sponges. Just west of the mooring is a towering pinnacle that reaches to within 50ft of the surface. Descend to the base of the pinnacle, where you will find a couple of small caves and swim-throughs. During certain times of the year (particularly in summer), some of the canyons are packed with schools of shimmering silversides. Large tarpon and jacks congregate in those areas, slowly picking away at the hoards of tiny fish. You'll probably see some large turtles and spotted eagle rays and perhaps even a reef shark.

About 150ft inshore from Orange Canyon is **Bonnie's Arch**, where an impressive coral arch spans a 30ft-wide tunnel. More tarpon and horse-eye jacks can be seen swimming about. Also look for filefish and friendly angelfish.

8 Big Tunnel

This site features a veritable maze of dramatic tunnels and swim-throughs, but its namesake tunnel is southwest of the mooring at about 100ft. You and several buddies can fit through it easily. It's best to follow the divemaster—the area is confusing and having a guide can be helpful. For reference, remember that all of the canyons run perpendicular to shore.

On the face of this vertical wall and on the pinnacles, you'll find a colorful collection of anemones, gorgonian sea fans, sea whips, and tube, barrel and elephant ear sponges. Black coral thrives deeper down

Location: Southeast of North West Point

Depth Range: 55-100ft (17-30m)

Access: Boat

Expertise Rating: Intermediate

the wall. Horse-eye and yellow jacks swim along the face and tarpon hang in the caves feeding on silversides. Look for stingrays in the sand and eagle rays and sharks in the blue waters beyond.

PIERCE & NEWMAN

In the Caymans, brown tube sponges grow in clusters and can be massive—up to several feet long.

9 Little Tunnels

Location: Northern West Bay

Depth Range: 58-100ft (18-30m)

Access: Boat

Expertise Rating: Intermediate

As you've probably guessed, the entire northwest reef structure is absolutely riddled with tunnels, making exploration a lot of fun. This site and the nearby **Big Dipper** site are spur-and-groove formations, which always run perpendicular to shore.

From the mooring buoy swim about 75ft to the opening of a short, narrow tunnel that cuts through the reef. The tunnel starts at 65ft and ends at 85ft. Look for a pinnacle nearby that rises up to about 80ft. Descend the sloping wall to a canopy of plate coral and thick carpet of encrusting sponges. The elephant ear and barrel sponges are massive, with some reaching 6ft in diameter. Watch for turtles and eagle rays. In the shallows, garden eels pop up out of the sand and solitary cornetfish usually sway among the gorgonians.

10 Round Rock

Location: Northern West Bay

Depth Range: 58-80ft (18-24m)

Access: Boat

Expertise Rating: Intermediate

Between two mooring balls is a broad, enormous coral pinnacle—the "round rock"—which you can easily navigate around, through and over. In fact, you don't really need to venture far from the mooring, as this singular site offers much to explore. The rock is cut with many swim-throughs, which you can easily weave in and out of, or you can simply hover above the mound to observe the marine life in action.

You'll find stunning formations of overlapping plate corals. In several places the coral overhangs resemble flying buttresses, extending from the ornate coral architecture. Also, bright orange elephant ear sponges encrust and protrude from the walls. These interesting sponges are found throughout the Caymans and

PIERCE & NEWMAN

Finger corals and swaying anemones decorate the pinnacle.

are unmistakable, due to their distinct coloring and convoluted, flat shapes. You'll see juvenile tropicals and schools of blue chromis swimming above the reef. Look for swaying garden eels in the sandy areas.

11 Trinity Caves

Don't worry, you won't need to be cave-certified to explore this area. These "caves" are actually narrow passageways leading through mountains of coral walls.

Three deep canyons, which run perpendicular to shore, begin at about 60ft and drop down to the edge of the wall at 100ft. If you follow the east canyon, you'll see a swim-through archway. Keep going until you reach the drop-off. Right at the drop-off is a beautiful soaring pinnacle with swaying gorgonians and plumes of black coral—you can't miss it. As you swim around the pinnacle, you'll find a tremendous number of

Location: Northern West Bay

Depth Range: 58-80ft (18-24m)

Access: Boat

Expertise Rating: Intermediate

sponges, including massive barrel and basket sponges. To get back to the mooring line, just follow any of the ravines back toward shore. The top of the wall features tall formations of swaying gorgonian whips.

Barrel sponges grow just a half-inch (1.25cm) per year, so large ones like this are quite old.

STEVE ROSENBERG

12 Silver Sands

Although it isn't dived much, this is an excellent spot, which lies within sight of the Silver Sands condos. The mostly spur-and-groove structure has some large coral mounds and features nice overhangs, swim-throughs and dead ends.

Spend some time looking around and under the coral mounds and shingle-like ledges. You might find lobsters, eels and slumbering nurse sharks. Check the sandy areas for hunting eagle rays.

This is a particularly pretty site with a surprising number of encrusting gorgonians. You'll see the bushy white mounds

Location: Northern West Bay

Depth Range: 30-50ft (9-15m)

Access: Boat

Expertise Rating: Novice

on the coral heads. As with pillar coral, the gorgonians' flowing hair-like polyps are extended during the daytime. If you're lucky, you might even spot the midnight parrotfish—a monster!

13 Aquarium

Get out your close-up and macro lenses, because this is the place to shoot fish. That said, you just might find a nurse shark as well. The structure here consists of wide coral fingers ("spurs") that top out at 30ft and drop to the sand at 45ft. Within sight of the mooring is a promi-

Location: West Bay

Depth Range: 35-50ft (11-15m)

Access: Boat

Expertise Rating: Novice

A bold French angelfish.

nent stand of pillar coral, about 7ft tall. This is one of the few types of coral that has its polyps exposed day and night. If you wave your hand near it, you'll see its tiny "hairs" flowing in the water. Within this "aquarium" are many species of reef fish, including gray and French angelfish, sergeant major, snapper and large grouper. You'll also see a lot of cleaning going on at the cleaning stations.

Look under overhangs along the edges of the fingers to find eels, spiny lobsters and grouper. You might also see the pretty goldentail moray—a brown eel covered with tiny yellow spots. Just two coral fingers south of the mooring line is a mini-ledge with an overhang, where divers frequently find nurse sharks. Aquarium is a popular night dive because of the shallow depth. Just north of Aquarium is another excellent shallow site called **Spanish Anchor**, where you can actually see—guess what?—an old Spanish anchor.

14 Governor's (Peter's) Reef

All divers will enjoy this shallow spot just offshore in the West Bay. Here you can watch fish and fish behavior to your heart's content, with plenty of bottom time and no stress.

Look for very big spotted grouper posing like great patriarchs. Occasionally they're seen hunting with eels—the grouper actually hovers right over the eel as it makes its way across the reef, stirring up a possible meal for its sharp-eyed companion. Bring a camera, because the photo opportunities for angelfish are excellent. These guys really know they're protected here, so

Location: West Bay

Depth Range: 35-50ft (11-15m)

Access: Boat

Expertise Rating: Novice

they get right up close to your mask. You'll see them all—French, gray and queen angelfish, as well as the yellow-and-black rock beauty. Look under ledges to find the elusive spotted drum, with its long flowing dorsal fin.

PIERCE & MORRISEY

No shortage of photo opportunities on Grand Cayman's West End.

15 *Oro Verde*

This 184ft vessel has been lying on the ocean floor since 1980, when local diving pioneer Bob Soto and companions sank it to create an artificial reef. According to the rumor mill, this was originally a Jamaican cargo vessel loaded with bales of *ganja*. Now it rests on the sandy bottom, somewhat battered and torn up. You can penetrate several sections easily, but watch out for sharp metal.

A lot of fish feeding goes on here, so marine life is abundant. You'll see Nassau grouper and speckled conies, beautiful angelfish, Bermuda chub, horse-eye and

Location: West Bay

Depth: 50ft (15m)

Access: Boat

Expertise Rating: Novice

yellow jacks, yellowtail snapper and the occasional barracuda. Look for moray eels inside the structure and garden eels and stingrays in the sand around the vessel.

To Feed or Not to Feed?

One of the joys of diving is that you get a ringside seat to the fascinating world beneath the waves. Have you ever tried simply hovering motionless over a coral head for several minutes? The spectacle is like a well-choreographed theater production—tiny gobies and shrimp busily work at their cleaning stations, sergeant majors protect their egg patches, parrotfish crunch on coral, scorpionfish and frogfish perch motionless, waiting for a

passing meal. If you come along with a handout—peas, Cheez Whiz, etc.—you miss all this activity. What's worse, you contribute toward altering fish behavior, and not for the better. In fact, some marine creatures can become downright belligerent if they're accustomed to being fed and don't get that expected meal.

So what about Stingray City? Well, stingrays in this area were being fed by humans long before Jacques Cousteau ever dreamed of the Aqua-Lung. Historically, fishing boats anchored in the shallow and protected North Sound to clean their catch, throwing the remains overboard. The stingrays in the area weren't stupid—when they heard the noise of the engines, they'd congregate and wait for lunch. Dive operators simply took this behavior a step further, dropping divers and snorkelers into waters where rays were already being fed.

PIERCE & NEWMAN

16 Hammerhead Hole

Alas, it's unlikely you'll see any hammerheads here but there is a chance you'll spot a nurse shark. This shallow site has nice coral spurs right around the mooring, so you won't need to stray far. Lobsters are plentiful, hunkered down into the holes among the corals. Turtles show up occasionally and you might spot stingrays in the sand. Mostly, though, this is a good site to take your time and appreciate the small stuff.

If you have your heart set on spotting sharks, ask the divemaster to take you south to about the fifth coral spur over. This long spur has cuts and grooves where nurse sharks like to sleep. Look for spotted eagle rays feeding in the sand nearby. It'll take about 12 minutes to swim out to the spur, so you should probably do this first, before returning to explore the area around the mooring.

Location: West Bay

Depth Range: 30-50ft (9-15m)

Access: Boat

Expertise Rating: Novice

STEVE ROSENBERG

Though rarely dangerous, nurse sharks may bite if provoked.

17 Rhapsody (Mesa)

Located just south of the *Oro Verde* wreck, this site is commonly called Mesa because of its high, flat-topped coral formation. Steep sides drop off sharply, forming a mini-wall. At the base of the wall, look for huge grouper getting spruced up at their cleaning stations. Twisting wire coral and several varieties of sponges cover the face. Individual coral heads spread out over the top of the mesa, where large concentrations of fish congregate.

You'll probably see schools of bluestriped grunts, silvery schoolmasters and

Location: West Bay

Depth Range: 30-50ft (9-15m)

Access: Boat

Expertise Rating: Novice

yellowtail snapper hanging out. The French and gray angelfish are especially gregarious here, so definitely bring a camera. Night diving at Rhapsody is, well, rhapsodic.

18 Royal Palms Ledge

This site, which is named after a resort that no longer exists, is fascinating and you'll have plenty of bottom time to explore it. A sandy horseshoe-shaped channel ranging from 6 to 8ft wide runs through the shallow coral. In many sections this channel is like a tunnel, due to the severely undercut coral mounds.

Location: West Bay

Depth Range: 30-50ft (9-15m)

Access: Boat

Expertise Rating: Novice

A rough fileclam has white or orange tentacles.

STEVE ROSENBERG

Finning along, you'll see large barrel sponges and schools of jack and snapper. As you follow the channel, look for an exceptionally large coral overhang—about 12 to 16ft tall. This creates a ceiling of coral where you can see fish swimming upside down. And it's a good spot to look for the little critters— white-tentacled clams, tiny blue shrimp, snails, tunicates and juvenile lobster.

19 *Balboa* & Cheeseburger Reef

Both of these sites lie right at the entrance to George Town Harbour and are surprisingly excellent areas to find a wide variety of marine life. Because they're accessible and shallow, they're also popular night dives.

The *Balboa* was a small freighter. It is now completely broken up and coral-encrusted, so penetration is not possible, at least for humans. Octopus, eel, lobster, crab and squid have no problem at all working their way inside.

Sections of Cheeseburger Reef are as shallow as 14ft, so this is a very good spot for snorkeling. Divers will find lots of swim-throughs and dead ends, overhangs

Location: George Town Harbour

Depth Range: 20-30ft (6-9m)

Access: Boat or shore

Expertise Rating: Novice

and nooks and crannies. Big tarpon congregate here, as well as a wide variety of small reef fish. You'll probably see schools of dark blue surgeonfish. Naturally, boat traffic is the downside here. Nevertheless, the reef is in surprisingly good shape. For safety, dive with an operator.

20 Eden Rock & Devil's Grotto

Welcome to grotto-land, boys and girls! Both of these superb shore-diving sites feature grottos and caverns aplenty, and because of the shallow depths, you won't have to hurry home. Snorkelers will have a super time here, too.

Location: South of George Town

Depth Range: 20-40ft (6-12m)

Access: Shore

Expertise Rating: Novice

Access couldn't be easier—the Eden Rock Diving Center can provide a map showing the underwater labyrinth. Divers should snorkel out to the buoys, then drop down and begin to explore. The caverns have plenty of light but bring a flashlight along to peer into all the crevices. Snorkelers can glide right over the caverns that divers explore and watch their bubbles escape from the Swiss cheese–like structures. You're likely to see schools of little silversides and shimmering silver tarpon.

21 Parrot's Reef

You'll find this lush reef about 90ft off the dock at Parrot's Landing Watersports Park. Just grab a tank or a snorkel, kick out beyond the volcanic rock ironshore and enjoy. It's teeming with marine life. As the name suggests, you'll find plenty of parrotfish—usually munching away at the mountainous star coral and brain coral—as well as angelfish, sergeant major, yellowtail snapper and French grunts. Barrel and tube sponges make

Location: South of George Town

Depth Range: 20-40ft (6-12m)

Access: Shore

Expertise Rating: Novice

good photo subjects. Come out at night to have fun with the octopuses.

STEVE ROSENBERG

The parrotfish uses its "beak" to scrape an algae meal off the coral.

22 Eagle Ray Rock

This is a dramatic site on the southern section of the West Wall, and it's a deep one. You'll actually negotiate your way through a canyon with soaring banks of coral on either side. As the site's name implies, the odds are good for seeing eagle rays cruising by. The reef here is healthy and loaded with sponges of all types, including good-sized barrel sponges.

In addition to extraordinary sponge life, which includes encrusting sponges and long branching rope sponges, expect to see wide-eyed balloonfish and gray and queen angelfish. Also look for garden eels in the sandy shallows.

Location: North of South West Point

Depth Range: 52-100ft (16-30m)

Access: Boat

Expertise Rating: Intermediate

Be Gentle with the Giants

If you think barrel sponges in the Caymans seem pretty big, you're right—some actually reach a diameter of more than 6ft (2m). Since they grow only a half-inch (1.25cm) per year, their size shows that these behemoths live longer than most of us landlubbers.

If you happen to see one that seems big enough to crawl into, definitely resist the temptation. Although sponges are generally pretty resilient, the lip of the sponge is rather delicate and can break easily. A broken lip can inhibit the sponge's ability to pump water into its inner chambers, which is how it feeds.

Remember, although they have no organs and don't move around, sponges are still members of the animal kingdom.

MICHAEL LAWRENCE

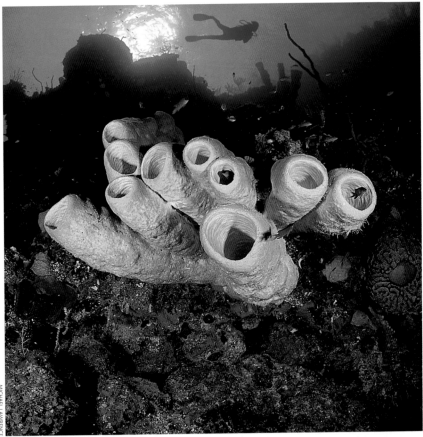

MICHAEL LAWRENCE

Brilliant yellow tube sponges attract small tropical fish such as these blackcap basslets.

23 Japanese Gardens

If you ask divemasters to name their favorite south shore sites, this one is usually high on the list. Its labyrinthine structure is a lot of fun and because it's shallow, you'll have plenty of time to play.

Venture down sand chutes, through cuts and into caverns. At certain times of the year, especially during the summer, the caves and caverns are filled with swirling masses of silversides, hungry bar jack and grouper. Swimthroughs are covered with soft corals and sponges. Expect to encounter morays and octopuses and don't be surprised if

Location: South Sound

Depth Range: 29-55ft (9-17m)

Access: Boat

Expertise Rating: Intermediate

you spot an eagle ray or nurse shark. Unfortunately, although it's considered one of the best shallow dives on Grand Cayman, the strong surge often keeps divemasters away.

East End Dive Sites

Craggy canyon walls soar high overhead as enormous sponges, mountainous star coral and bushes of black coral form a canopy over narrow sandy channels, reducing divers to diminutive proportions. The scale at these East End sites will make you feel positively Lilliputian. You'll also feel fortunate—not only are the sites intricate, exciting and complex, they're pristine and it's unlikely you'll see another dive boat at any location. This is the windward side—it's exposed to the northeast trade winds and more likely to experience high surf and currents—so most of the dive sites are clustered on the somewhat sheltered northeast and southeast areas.

In the southeast, a barrier reef extends around the south side to the tip of the East End. The area around East Point itself is usually rough, with high swells. Like the West Bay, the northeast lacks a fringing reef and features a shallower wall. Marine life, however, is more abundant. You'll notice lots of gorgonians, soft coral, black coral and sponges, especially elephant ear sponges.

Along most of the East End, the top of the wall is deep—it tops off at around 60 to 80ft (18 to 24m). Pelagic life cruises by the sheer face and around huge pinnacles. That said, the region's canyon-like terrain makes even the shallow reefs exciting.

Visitors will find nice lodgings on this serene end of the island, although the choices are limited. If you're staying on the West End, you can drive to East End dive operations in 30 to 45 minutes.

Grand Cayman East End Dive Sites	Good Snorkeling	Novice	Intermediate	Advanced
24 Ironshore Gardens		●		
25 Playing Field		●		
26 The Maze			●	
27 McKennedy's Canyon			●	
28 Pat's Wall			●	
29 Scuba Bowl			●	
30 Grouper Grotto		●		
31 Snapper Hole		●		
32 Babylon			●	

PIERCE & NEWMAN

At East End sites, canyon walls soar high overhead.

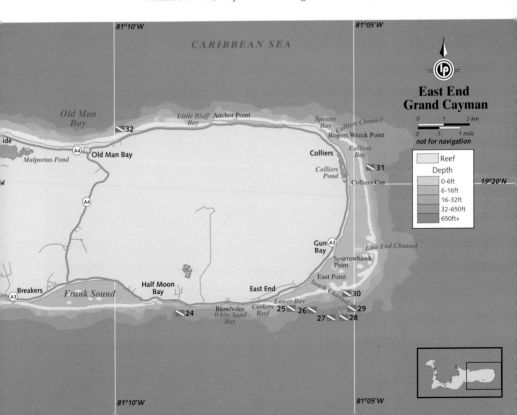

CARIBBEAN SEA

81°10'W

81°05'W

**East End
Grand Cayman**

0   1   2 km
0   .5   1 mile
not for navigation

Reef

Depth

0-6ft

6-16ft

16-32ft

32-650ft

650ft+

19°20'N

Old Man
Bay

Little Bluff   Anchor Point
Bay

Spotter
Bay   Colliers Channel

Rogers Wreck Point

32

ide

Malportas Pond   Old Man Bay

A4

Colliers   Colliers
Bay

Colliers
Pond

31

N

A4

Colliers Cay

Gun   A3
Bay

East End Channel

Sparrowhawk
Point

East Point

East End

South Channel

30

Breakers

Frank Sound

Half Moon
Bay

A3

Lower Bay

25   29

Corkers   26
Reef

24

Blowholes
White Sand
Bay

27   28

81°10'W

81°05'W

24 Ironshore Gardens

In this shallow environment, you'll see thick clusters of golden elkhorn coral reaching toward the sun and silvery yellow-tailed schoolmasters hovering beneath the branches.

Location: Southeast of Half Moon Bay

Depth Range: 30-50ft (9-15m)

Access: Boat

Expertise Rating: Novice

Beyond the shallows is canyon-like terrain. Most of the southeast part of the island is riddled with caves and winding tunnels—stunning underwater territory with a tremendous amount to see. It would be unusual not to find schools of steely tarpon swimming in formation in these canyons. If you're swimming at the base of a passageway underneath one of these schools, look up for an impressive view.

PIERCE & NEWMAN

The dorsal "eyes" of the foureye butterflyfish serve as protective decoys, tempting predators to strike at the rear instead of at the head.

25   Playing Field

Location: Southeast of Lower Bay

Depth Range: 30-50ft (9-15m)

Access: Boat

Expertise Rating: Novice

Although this is mostly patch reef, it's also still very canyon-like in structure, and incredibly lush and healthy—truly a perfect "field" for playing. Fish feeding is particularly discouraged on the East End, so you'll see more natural fish behavior. Expect to find schooling grunts, chub and Creole wrasse. Also look for butterflyfish, cornetfish and French angelfish.

If you're after some nice photographs of the beautiful French angelfish, you're in luck. Look for them wherever you find sponges, especially the encrusting kind, which are common in the Caymans. The angelfish's diet consists primarily of sponges, but also includes some gorgonians, tunicates and other invertebrate life.

Although the French angelfish is shy, it's also curious. If you approach it very cautiously, you should be able to click off some nice shots. To get a good shot, focus your camera on the angelfish's distinctive yellow-ringed eyes, which will probably be looking directly at you.

Little Angels

The coloring of the juvenile French angelfish is completely different than that of the adult. The juvenile has a similar shape (though smaller, of course) but is completely black with five vertical bright yellow stripes. As the fish matures, the stripes fade and gold crescents emerge on the edges of the scales. The juvenile French angelfish is easily confused with the juvenile gray angelfish as they have similar coloring. To tell them apart, look closely at their tails. The French (both adult and juvenile) has a rounded tail, while the gray has a square-cut tail. Also, the French juvenile's tail is black with yellow markings around its oval border. The gray juvenile has yellow bar on its foretail and is white or transparent along the very end.

juvenile French angelfish

mature French angelfish

26 The Maze

Although the top of the reef starts at about 40ft, the wall tops out deeper

Location: South of East Point

Depth Range: 40-100ft (12-30m)

Access: Boat

Expertise Rating: Intermediate

STEVE ROSENBERG

A diver can't see the black coral for the trees.

at 65ft, so this site is recommended for more experienced divers.

You'll find a virtual playground of zigzagging passageways, with canyon walls that soar like skyscrapers. Follow the sand ravines out to the drop-off, where you shouldn't be surprised to come across a selection of pelagic life. You might find spotted eagle rays and sharks—Caribbean reef, blacktip or bull. If you're really lucky you might even spot migrating whales here.

Explore the main wall and the several large pinnacles, which are adorned with a rainbow-colored blur of healthy sponges and corals, including trees of black coral.

27 McKennedy's Canyon

This one starts very deep, so your bottom time will be severely limited. Don't forget to watch your air and depth gauges, because you will certainly be distracted. Aside from its incredible canyon-like terrain cracked with tunnels and swim-throughs, the site is notable for its enormous lavender sea fans—up to 4ft tall—and giant yellow and brown tube sponges. If you examine the sea fans closely, you can find a flamingo tongue, an orange-spotted mollusc that attaches itself to and feeds upon gorgonians.

Location: Southeast of East Point

Depth Range: 60-100ft (18-30m)

Access: Boat

Expertise Rating: Intermediate

On the other end of the marine spectrum, you might also spot black-tipped reef sharks, which occasionally cruise by.

28 Pat's Wall

Named after a local divemaster, Pat's Wall features many narrow, deep channels. Like most of the sites hugging the East End, this is exciting and dramatic canyon country. This site is particularly lush, with bushy purplish sea plumes and deep-water sea fans. You'll find sea whips and black coral as well. Evidently, storms and hurricanes don't do much damage at these depths, as the coral is in beautiful condition. The tops of the coral heads begin at about 70ft and plummet

Location: Southeast of East Point

Depth Range: 60-100ft (18-30m)

Access: Boat

Expertise Rating: Intermediate

to between 100 and 150ft. But that's nothing—the other side of the wall descends 6,000ft.

29 Scuba Bowl

Just outside the South Channel, Scuba Bowl is like a structural slalom course, winding in, out and around craggy coral cuts leading to the main wall. It's a lot of fun, but the depths don't leave much time to play.

You'll see enormous deep-water gorgonian fans branching out into the blue water to catch little critters in the current. Colorful encrusting sponges and groups of brown tube sponges, as well as glistening green leaf-like algae, decorate the wall

Location: Southeast of East Point

Depth Range: 77-100ft (23-30m)

Access: Boat

Expertise Rating: Intermediate

and pinnacles. Here and at neighboring sites you just might get lucky and see a reef shark casually cruising by.

Sponge communities provide shelter for many of the reef's tiny creatures.

30 Grouper Grotto

This shallow site has a tabletop structure with corals coming right up to within 20ft of the surface. You'll find thick stands of elkhorn coral as well as sea fans, sea whips and boulders of brain coral. Just off the ledge of the "table" is typical East End canyon-like terrain with massive cuts and coral buttresses.

Ubiquitous schools of silversides gather in these overhead structures and wherever they happen to be. Also expect to see their ever-present predator, the tarpon. Schools of tarpon occasionally herd the baitfish into a tight ball

Location: Southeast of East Point

Depth Range: 25-50ft (8-15m)

Access: Boat

Expertise Rating: Novice

before darting in for the catch. Don't confuse tarpon with barracuda, a common mistake. Both are sleek, silver and shimmering, but tarpon have much bigger eyes and scales, a forked tail and an upturned mouth. Also, you won't see a tarpon's teeth, whereas a barracuda's teeth are very obvious.

Tarpon Tales

Tarpon (*Megalops atlanticus*) are long, silvery fish that are distinguished by their upturned mouths. Because of their size—up to 8ft (2m) in length—and their upright dorsal fins, divers sometimes mistake them for sharks. Tarpon are renowned game fish and known for their tremendous fighting ability when hooked. Luckily for them, tarpon meat is definitely not worth trying. A female tarpon lays 13 million eggs in a single spawn, but very few of these eggs survive to become fully grown. During they day, you will often see tarpon in large schools, swimming slowly around reefs, seagrass areas, canals and other secluded areas.

LAWSON WOOD

—*Reef Line*, the newsletter of Reef Relief

31 Snapper Hole

This site offers excellent shallow diving and deep diving as well. The shallow reef hosts schools of Bermuda chub, tarpon and, of course, snapper. The reef itself is a maze of tunnels, caverns and cuts with massive numbers of silversides, which in turn attract tarpon.

The coral is pristine, including a tall spire of pillar coral. Look for pelagics:

Location: East of Colliers Bay

Depth Range: 36-65ft (11-20m)

Access: Boat

Expertise Rating: Novice

you might see eagle rays and the occasional shark—usually a blacktip or nurse shark. Also look for the anchor from the wreck of the *Methusalem,* a broken-up tanker.

You're certain to see plenty of snapper here and on almost every other dive you make in the Caymans. They're distinguished by their silvery color, sloping heads and tapered bodies. In these islands you'll usually see the yellowtail variety as well as schoolmasters. Yellowtail have a brilliant yellow stripe running the length of the body and, of course, a yellow tail. To confuse matters, schoolmasters also have yellow tails. They don't, however, have the yellow stripe and all of their fins are yellow, not just the tail.

STEVE ROSENBERG

Schoolmasters have yellow fins, but not the yellowtail's stripe.

32 Babylon

You'll have a great time at this very popular site on the Northeast Wall. First, kick out to the wall itself, then take a left and you'll run into a huge solitary pinnacle. Between the pinnacle and the wall you'll find black coral in profusion—in fact, there are several different types here. Babylon features the East End's standard cuts and canyons along the top of the wall, which abounds with multicolored rope sponges, barrel sponges and huge sea fans. Expect to find schools of

Location: North shore, east of Old Man Bay

Depth Range: 55-100ft (17-30m)

Access: Boat

Expertise Rating: Intermediate

black durgon and creole wrasse on top of the reef.

STEVE ROSENBERG

A diver hovers near Babylon's swaying gorgonians.

Cayman Brac Dive Sites

Cayman Brac is a real treat for divers of all levels. You'll find high visibility—50ft is considered a bad day—and little current. Cruise ships keep their distance as there is very little safe harbor. Plus, there is little industry or development to cause dirt runoff, so the reef is pristine. Strangely, the Brac's dives sites—and even the island itself—have not received the attention and respect they truly deserve. Considering the unabated growth on Grand Cayman, this is probably a good thing.

Fringing reef surrounds most of the island. Because of its torpedo-like shape, the Brac has two separate diving environments—north and south. The east and west tips of the islands receive the strongest currents. Winds usually come in from the east, however, so the West End is somewhat more protected.

Perfect for both snorkeling and diving, the Brac's shallow sites are as spectacular as those along the wall. Coral heads frequently reach to just 10 to 20ft below the surface. You'll find a lot of overlapping plate and lettuce coral, as well as pillar and mountainous star coral.

Dive operations are found mostly on the south shore of the West End. Most dive sites are just minutes away from shore, so you'll suit up as soon as you get on

Cayman Brac Dive Sites	Good Snorkeling	Novice	Intermediate	Advanced
33 Patch Reef		●		
34 Cemetery Wall			●	
35 Garden Eel Wall			●	
36 MV *Capt. Keith Tibbetts*	●	●		
37 *Cayman Mariner*		●		
38 The Chutes		●	●	
39 Airport Reef		●	●	
40 Sergeant Major Reef		●		
41 Wilderness Wall (Cio's Craig)			●	
42 Rock Monster Chimney		●		
43 Bert Brothers Boulders		●		
44 Radar Reef		●		

the boat. East End sites require a slightly longer boat ride, but they're spectacular and well worth the effort. Cayman Brac dive operations also schedule trips to Little Cayman's Bloody Bay Marine Park, about 45 minutes away.

Altogether, the Brac has about 45 moored sites. Though buoys bob all around the island, most Brac diving is on the calmer northwest side. Off the north shore, a mini-wall starts at about 20 to 30ft (6 to 9m) and drops to a ledge at 50ft (15m). Beyond this ledge is the sloping main wall, which starts at 50 to 60ft (15 to 18m) and descends to 4,000ft (1,200m). Several huge sandy chutes spill down over the rim. The wall extends all the way around the island, but the north has more sponge life than the south, including large barrel, strawberry and vase sponges.

In the south, spur-and-groove coral formations run perpendicular to the shore, making navigation easy. The main wall starts at 60 to 70ft (18 to 21m)—about 10ft (3m) deeper than the north side—and plunges to about 1,000ft (300m). Southern dive sites are impressive—with plenty of tunnels and chimneys, they somewhat resemble the topside limestone cliffs.

PIERCE & MORRISEY

On the Brac, dive sites are just minutes from shore.

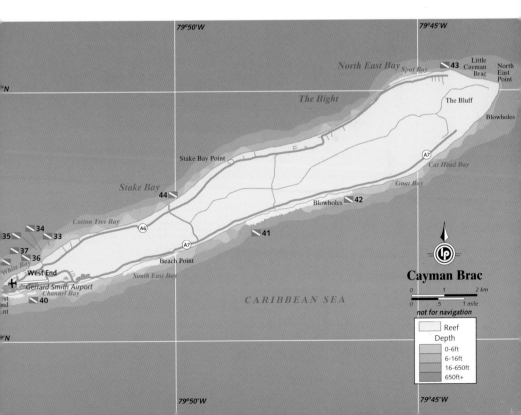

33 Patch Reef

As the name implies, the coral structure here is patch reef. The reef consists mostly of mountainous star coral—both the mound and sheet variety—which decorates the shallow sandy bottom. Pufferfish, friendly angelfish and schools of grunts, as well as large numbers of juvenile tropicals regularly hang out here. This is a great spot to find the little creatures that often get overlooked, such as the elusive sailfin blenny. Although these guys won't stay long if you approach, they're unmistakable with their long dorsal fins that look like sails.

Watch for cleaning stations where shrimp and wrasse provide efficient

Location: Cotton Tree Bay

Depth Range: 30-50ft (9-15m)

Access: Boat

Expertise Rating: Novice

hygienic services to grouper and other large fish cruising by, getting a free meal in return. Watch the cleaner busily clean its guest's entire body, pecking at parasites and dead tissue, and occasionally disappearing into the cavernous mouth to clean away fearlessly, only to pop out of the gills brazenly. If you're taking pictures here, be sure to use your close-up or macro lens.

Cleaning Stations

STEVE ROSENBERG

A tiger grouper gets a cleaning from an eager pair of wrasse.

Observant divers will discover a variety of symbiotic relationships—associations in which two dissimilar organisms participate in a mutually beneficial relationship—throughout the marine world. One of the most interesting symbiotic relationships is found at cleaning stations, where one animal advertises its grooming services to potential clients with a series of inviting undulating movements.

Cleaner species may include wrasse, shrimp, angelfish, butterflyfish or tang. Their customers hover in line until their turn comes. When the cleaner attends to a waiting customer—perhaps a grouper, parrotfish or even moray eel—it is often seen entering the customer's mouth to perform dental hygiene, and may even exit through the fish's gills. Although the customer could have an easy snack, it would never swallow the essential cleaner. The large fish benefits from the removal of parasites and dead tissue, while the little cleaner is provided with a "free" meal.

Divers will find that if they approach a cleaning station carefully, they'll be able to get closer to more fish than is normally possible and will observe behavior seen nowhere else on the reef.

34 Cemetery Wall

Do you like walls? Dramatic steep drop-offs? Good, because that's what you'll get here. And don't worry—the cemetery in the name refers to the one directly on-shore.

The shore entry is on the north shore, just east of Tibbetts Square and the airport. From the north shore road, turn onto Cemetery Road and follow it to the end. Entry is from either side of the jetty but be careful on the sharp ironshore. You'll see mooring buoys for **Garden Eel Wall**, directly in front of the jetty, and **Charlie's Reef** and Cemetery Wall to the east. Charlie's Reef is a nice shallow site highlighting plenty of juveniles in addition to Charlie, a large green moray. On all these sites you'll encounter a spur-and-groove system with wide sandy channels. The maximum depth is 60ft until the wall drops off.

At Cemetery Wall, follow the coral patches and finger coral, at a depth of about 50 to 65ft, out to the main wall drop-off. On your way out, you'll start to see the swirling circular patterns characteristic of the Brac's plate coral. Plates overlap sandy chutes, creating a nice protected habitat for solitary tropicals.

As you follow the wide, sandy groove out to the wall, look for stingrays in the sand. Occasionally you might see a bar jack hunting with a sting-ray—the jack always hovers just overhead and is some-times nearly enveloped in the folds of the ray's "wings."

Location: Cotton Tree Bay

Depth Range: 50-100ft (15-30m)

Access: Boat or shore

Expertise Rating: Intermediate

The wall itself features an incredible array of healthy coral and sponges, including exquisite basket sponges and deep-water gorgonians. If you take a right and cross over the sand chutes, you might see sharks, turtles and eagle rays. The sand chutes tumble down, right over the wall. Look for a tunnel at 90ft—it will lead you right back to the top of the wall.

A green moray enjoys a good cleaning from a friend.

PIERCE & MORRISEY

35 Garden Eel Wall

This is a beautiful wall dive, with soaring coral pinnacles and lots of barrel and tube sponges, sea fans, sea whips and hard corals clinging to the wall. Expect to see very friendly angelfish and curious barracuda. Look for southern stingrays in the shallows. Watch for their outlines in the sand, as they frequently bury themselves completely, leaving only their eyes peeking out. Of course, you'll also see colonies of garden eels—these teeny little critters

Location: North of White Bay

Depth Range: 65-100ft (20-30m)

Access: Boat

Expertise Rating: Intermediate

anchored in the sand look more like blades of grass than marine animals.

36 MV *Capt. Keith Tibbetts*

In 1996, a Russian frigate (#356) was brought to the Brac from Cuba to finish its days as a diving attraction for Cayman Brac. Renamed after a pioneering local seaman, it was sunk with great fanfare. The entire ship can be seen easily from the surface, so it's a good spot for divers and snorkelers alike.

The massive gray structure—330ft long and 68ft high—lies in a roughly north-south direction and sits in 60ft. It rests on white sand, listing a bit to the port side. The turret guns, both fore and aft, are impressive sights and very good

Location: West of White Bay

Depth Range: 40-90ft (12-27m)

Access: Boat

Expertise Rating: Novice

photo subjects—definitely use a wide-angle lens.

The ship already shows many signs of deterioration. The cooling tower has toppled over and the ship has sunk a

RONALD STOLFA

The *Tibbetts*, a Cold War–era Russian frigate, is Cayman Brac's premier diving attraction.

good 15 to 20ft into the sand. Dangerous sections are closed off but you can safely enter the pilot-house, which leads down into the wreck, as well as the bridge and upper decks. Watch out for sharp, rusty metal and prickly sea urchins. In fact, it's a good idea to keep touching to a minimum. You can safely explore the bridge and upper decks. You'll probably see barracuda, queen angelfish and yellow tang milling about. A small reef area is off the starboard side in about 50ft. Otherwise, the entire area is a sandy plain—a perfect home for garden eels.

Other dive boats will probably be tied off at the site—there are three buoys—so be careful not to return to the wrong boat!

MICHAEL LAWRENCE

The *Tibbetts'* turret guns make a striking photo subject.

Artificial Reefs

The best way for divers to understand reef evolution is to observe artificial reefs at different stages of development. An artificial reef can be established with almost any submerged foreign object—most often it will be a ship or plane wreck, but also "junk" like tires, bottles or even concrete blocks. Broken-up wrecks offer an excellent chance to see marine life and are often worth at least a couple of dives.

The abundance of marine life and coral growth on an artificial reef depends on three main factors:

- **Location** Both natural and artificial reefs shelter animals from currents and from predators. Artificial reefs in open, sandy areas—like the *Tibbetts*—become an oasis for surrounding marine life. In current-swept locations, wrecks often attract species that are otherwise rare. Juvenile fish commonly take refuge in artificial reefs, while hydroids and sponges often attract an abundant nudibranch population.

- **Material** Steel generally provides an easy surface for coral to grow on. Rubber and aluminum objects, though they may provide excellent shelter, are more difficult for coral to attach to.

- **Age** Generally, coral takes at least a few years to establish itself. As the coral becomes more profuse, other species gradually move in. The longer the object has been underwater, the more populated and interesting the artificial reef becomes.

37 *Cayman Mariner*

This 55ft wreck is located inshore at a north side site called the East Chute, not far from the *Tibbetts*. Scuttled in 1986, the *Mariner* sits upright on the sand at about 60ft. You can venture into the hull and wheelhouse safely and easily. Inside you'll find brilliant red and orange encrusting sponges. Look up and notice the mirror effect of the air pockets that collect on the ceiling. Peek through the porthole or use it to frame a nice photo. Look for eels—they love to make their homes in wrecks. With luck you might see a moray enjoying a cleaning from a banded coral shrimp.

Location: North of West Bay

Depth Range: 50-60ft (15-18m)

Access: Boat

Expertise Rating: Novice

PIERCE & MORRISEY

Artificial reefs provide ideal habitats for marine life, such as this French angelfish.

38 **The Chutes**

The Chutes—**West Chute, Middle Chute** and **East Chute**—are popular dive spots located just east of Airport Reef. Each of the three sites has a similar dive plan—you'll start in the sandy shallows (look for rays here) and as you get a little deeper you'll see a sand chute flanked by high coral spurs. Follow the sandy chute as it slopes down to the

Location: North of the airport

Depth Range: 55-100ft (17-30m)

Access: Boat

Expertise Rating: Novice to Intermediate

wall's edge. Curious grouper are often found along the wall and you'll see giant barrel and tube sponges. East Chute is particularly alive with marine life and is where you'll find the *Cayman Mariner*. At East Chute you'll also find an old Spanish anchor embedded in coral at 90ft.

Graceful sea fans punctuate the underwater landscape.

39 Airport Reef

Just off the western tip of the island, this dive site is a double treat, offering both a nice shallow dive and a good deep wall dive. There's a mooring buoy on the reef side at 32ft and another on the wall at 60ft. The wall starts at about 65ft and slopes to around 100ft, where it takes a terrific plunge straight down into the deep.

Location: North of West End Point

Depth Range: 32-100ft (10-30m)

Access: Boat

Expertise Rating: Novice to Intermediate

You'll see an array of yellow and orange tube sponges protruding from the wall, especially in the large crevices. You might see schools of jacks and grunts. Grouper, blue-spotted conies and angelfish are also common. Night dives are nice on the shallow reef, where you're likely to spot octopuses. They'll change colors as they slither along the sand over rock and coral, and even over your hands.

PIERCE & NEWMAN
Shy octopuses rarely appear in the daytime.

40 Sergeant Major Reef

This site and nearby Butterfly Reef (a bit to the east) are fun spur-and-groove environments, with the coral heads topping off at about 25 to 30ft. Navigation is easy—as you wander around, keep a mental count of how many fingers ("spurs") you cross over, then make sure you come back over the same number.

Location: South of Channel Bay

Depth Range: 32-50ft (10-15m)

Access: Boat

Expertise Rating: Novice

While you're in the shallow depths, check out the beautiful golden-brown elkhorn coral, which usually attracts schooling fish. This coral is shallow enough that you'll see some storm damage. A profusion of staghorn coral lies a little deeper.

As you follow the spurs into deeper water, you'll come to some swim-throughs and several porthole-like coral openings. Look in small crevices for spiny lobsters and eels, and under ledges and inside caves for nurse sharks. Small turtles might be on or under the ledges. You'll probably see pufferfish, triggerfish, butterflyfish and blue tang, and the grouper in the area always seem to be getting cleaned. You're likely to see stingrays and spotted eagle rays foraging for food in the nice white sand between the fingers of coral.

A diver watches a group of schoolmasters congregate on a Cayman reef.

41 Wilderness Wall (Cio's Craig)

The pure white sand in the shallows here resembles an enchanted Alpine meadow, snow-covered and untouched. From the top of the reef, you can "slide" down one of several tunnels, some of which have soaring chimneys that slope through the wall. The tunnels will deposit you on the face of the wall anywhere from about 80 to 100ft.

Location: South of Beach Point

Depth Range: 46-100ft (14-30m)

Access: Boat

Expertise Rating: Intermediate

A huge round pinnacle—about 40ft in diameter—rises away from the wall to within 100ft of the surface, attracting pelagics and schools of horse-eye and yellow jacks. You'll also see Nassau grouper, angelfish, snapper and perhaps turtles and stingrays. The sponges are huge and come in mosaic patterns of red, yellow, orange, purple and green.

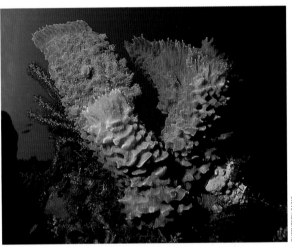

STEVE ROSENBERG

A striking azure vase sponge adds vibrant color to the reef.

42 Rock Monster Chimney

It is said that this site's name refers to the monstrous caves within the bluff that towers 160ft over the indigo blue water, but it could just as well refer to the monster of a reef underwater. This East End site's windward location results in nutrient-rich waters, which foster a very healthy reef. Unfortunately, the location limits your chances to dive because of frequently rough seas.

As you head out to the wall, you'll pass mostly over patch reefs. Rays like to forage in the sandy spaces between the coral patches. Look for little puffs of sand in

Location: South of Pollard Bay

Depth Range: 55-100ft (17-30m)

Access: Boat

Expertise Rating: Novice

the distance—they are a good indication that the rays are busy at their sandy dinner table. As you approach the wall, look for a vertical swim-through coral chimney east of the mooring. Inside you'll feel downright diminutive. Healthy soft corals and sponges blanket the wall at the drop-off and down the wall, and scal-loped plate corals create overhangs and ledges. This is a very sheer drop-off, so watch your depth carefully.

43 Bert Brothers Boulders

This site is named after islanders long involved in Brac diving. Though a local favorite, it is not much visited by boats because of its distance from the dive operations. The reef is pristine, consisting of spur-and-groove coral heads grouped together tightly and separated by narrow alleys of sand. Golden elkhorn coral shimmers in the shallow waters.

Access from shore is fairly easy—from Spot Bay, along the north shore road, look for a crafts store called NIM Things. Follow the road directly opposite it and park in front of the boat ramp. Walk down the ramp and head out to the

Location: Spot Bay

Depth Range: 20-60ft (6-18m)

Access: Boat or shore

Expertise Rating: Novice

mooring ball (at 20ft) just east of the ramp. You'll find a pristine spur-and-groove system with lots of ledges and overhangs—a perfect structure for finding eel and lobster. Also look for jawfish in the rubble at about 45ft.

Elkhorn coral grows rapidly—up to 6 inches (15cm) per year—but tends to be fragile.

The intricate structure and shallow depths are ideal for close-up or wide-angle photography. If you have a good macro setup look for tiny jawfish that live in the shallow rubble. They're skittish and difficult to photograph. With patience, however, you can get a shot when they pop up out of their sandy burrows.

44 Radar Reef

With easy access and shallow depths, this Stake Bay site offers one of the nicest shore dives on the island. You'll find plenty to look at both day and night, even if you stay above 30ft. In fact, at night you'll probably be happy to stay right around the jetty—its rocks and ledges are a haven for spiny lobster and night shrimp.

Location: Stake Bay

Depth Range: 15-60ft (5-18m)

Access: Boat or shore

Expertise Rating: Novice

To get to the shore entrance from the north shore road turn onto Kirkconnell Road, just east of the Cayman Brac Museum, and follow it to the end. Steps lead into the water from a jetty. Drop down after you get to the end of the jetty, turn east and look for an underwater cable that leads out to the reef.

If you arrive by boat, you'll find the mooring buoy in 25ft. The long stretch of phone cable that extends just east of the jetty out to sea attracts little critters, including banded coral shrimp, arrow crabs, lettuce leaf slugs and juvenile fish—a perfect macro setup. Sea fans and gorgonians on coral spurs bend in the surge and eagle rays and squid feed in the sandy grooves. Visit at night to see sleeping parrotfish, wandering octopuses, spiny lobster and shrimp.

STEVE ROSENBERG

Look near the mooring buoy for small critters like the arrow crab.

Little Cayman Dive Sites

What draws divers to Little Cayman? In a word: walls—incredible walls. The walls in Little Cayman's waters drop hundreds of feet so vertically they'll make you gasp in your regulator. Bloody Bay Marine Park is the legendary home to these wonders. The marine park encompasses about 22 mooring sites along the northwest shore, spanning both Bloody and Jackson's bays. The shallow tops of these walls—some come to just 20ft (6m) from the surface—are nearly as incredible as their depths. This makes for long bottom times and enjoyable safety stops.

To avoid stressing the popular Bloody Bay sites, diving in the marine park is limited to two 20-diver boats per day. Conditions on the north shore can be rough—another limiting factor. Luckily, there are some 57 moored sites around the island, so even if you're "blown out" of the north shore you'll have plenty of other diving options.

When the north shore gets too rough, dive boats head south. The south wall crests deeper than in the north—50 to 80ft (15 to 24m)—but it is not nearly as precipitous. The shallow reefs on this side are pristine and the walls host colorful sponge communities, particularly tube, rope and enormous barrel sponges. As on all the islands, marine life is protected, abundant and unabashedly fearless. Fish feeding is discouraged.

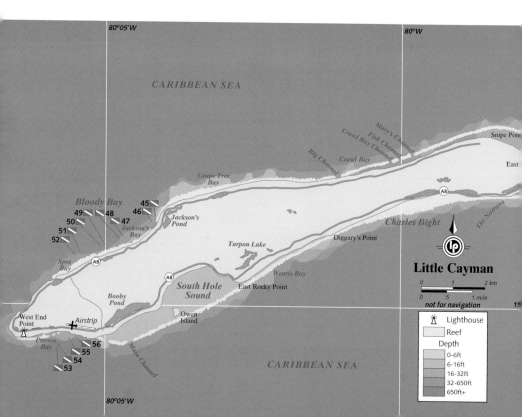

Little Cayman Dive Sites

	Good Snorkeling	Novice	Intermediate	Advanced
45 Eagle Ray Roundup			●	
46 Cumber's Caves	●		●	
47 Mixing Bowl (Three-Fathom Wall)	●		●	
48 Marilyn's Cut (Hole in the Wall)			●	
49 Randy's Gazebo (Chimney)			●	
50 Great Wall East & West			●	
51 Coconut Wall (Coconut Grove)			●	
52 Barracuda Bite			●	
53 Patty's Place				●
54 Richard's Reef		●		
55 Gay's Reef		●		
56 Wind Sock Reef		●		

45　Eagle Ray Roundup

In addition to a sloping wall, this section of reef in Jackson's Bay also features open, shallow sandy areas surrounded by large coral formations. This sandy amphitheater attracts a lot of interesting

Location: West of Jackson's Bay

Depth Range: 29-100ft (9-30m)

Access: Boat

Expertise Rating: Intermediate

STEVE ROSENBERG

An eagle ray soars gracefully through the water.

marine life including, of course, eagle rays and stingrays. Divers who prefer to stay shallow can have a lot of fun without going over the wall.

Just before the wall's drop-off, the reef is only about 40ft deep. Several sandy chutes run through the reef, sloping down the wall. At the beginning of the drop-off, you'll see a profusion of gorgonians, including lacy sea fans. Bright purple and orange tube and barrel sponges protrude from the wall, while schools of blue chromis parade up and over the reef in formation. The wall here is more sloping than at Bloody Bay and, since it's relatively shallow, you'll have plenty of time to explore.

On the reef you'll see blue parrotfish—usually munching on brain coral—and a surprising number of cleaning stations. While exploring the sandy areas, look for swaying garden eels. Also look for colonies of jawfish hovering above their burrows. They spook easily, but if you approach cautiously, you might see one of the males incubating a mouthful of eggs.

Yellowhead Jawfish: An Ideal Husband

STEVE ROSENBERG

The yellowhead jawfish is named in part for its big mouth, which is often used as a shovel to dig its nest, a hole in the sandy bottom or coral rubble area near a reef. The male jawfish is an unusually good father. He waits in his burrow for a visiting female and then carries her eggs in his mouth to protect them from harm, especially when they hatch. If you're lucky, you will see a proud father poke his head out from his hole, look around furtively and, when the coast is clear, open his mouth to let his children out to "play." When danger threatens—*slurp!*—into the mouth go the children, and down the hole goes the jawfish.
—From *Reef Line*, the newsletter of Reef Relief

46　Cumber's Caves

The beauty of the sites along Jackson's Bay is their incredible versatility. This one is perfect for both boat and shore diving; for night diving and for snorkeling; and for both novice divers and experienced deep divers—everyone's happy! As a shore dive, the entry is very easy and even though it's a good distance to the mooring buoy, most of it is over shallow sand and rock, so you can actually walk out for a long way.

If you like cuts and swim-throughs, you'll really like this wall. Tunnels wind through the structure, penetrating the

Location: West of Jackson Bay

Depth Range: 20-100ft (6-30m)

Access: Boat or shore

Expertise Rating: Intermediate

reef all along its length. First, you'll fin across a sandy plain—yep, look for rays—to the reef section at about 45ft. Find a cut in the wall and right in front of the cut an anchor wedged in the sand. Keep your fins up, so as not to stir the sand as you fall down into the "cave," which descends at about a 40- to 45-degree angle. Several openings above allow light rays to shine onto the sponge and coral-encrusted walls. You'll curve around a bit as you head down, then see the blue beyond as you exit at about 85ft.

In this deeper section you'll likely see plenty of sea fans, rope sponges and basket sponges. As you make your way up the wall back to the shallow sandy area, there are many more opportunities to explore shallow cuts and swim-throughs. Novice divers should stay around the sand and reef area, which is home to rays, garden eels, jawfish, conch and anemones.

47　Mixing Bowl (Three-Fathom Wall)

This site marks the division between Jackson's Bay and Bloody Bay. On the Jackson's Bay side of the site, the wall angles out and a wide, sandy channel runs parallel to shore and just inside the wall. Here, the top of the wall is only three fathoms (18ft), so it's a great shallow dive and snorkel site.

Location: Between Jackson's Bay and Bloody Bay

Depth Range: 18-100ft (5-30m)

Access: Boat

Expertise Rating: Intermediate

More experienced divers can descend a winding sandy corridor on the Bloody Bay section, which has a much steeper drop-off than the Jackson's Bay portion. Pass over a brilliant white sandy slope (be careful not to stir it up), which slices right through the reef side at a 45-degree angle. You can follow this down to 100ft. Now get ready for an incredible sight—a patchwork quilt of colors completely covering the wall with purple, brilliant white, orange and red sponges. Cuts and canyons gouge the wall itself, creating more swim-throughs and habitats. You cannot miss the yellowfin

PIERCE & NEWMAN

Gorgonian fans and vase sponges cover the wall at Jackson's Bay.

grouper—they're huge and healthy. Also keep an eye out for the little stuff—frogfish (usually on sponges) and even seahorses.

If you're finning on top of the wall and feel like you're being watched, you're probably right. Large friendly grouper will sidle right up, practically begging for attention. They'll stay perfectly still while you stroke their silky sides—you half-expect them to start purring. Here you'll see many schools of fish: jacks, chromis, schoolmasters, grunts and snappers. To complete the total sensual overload, there's even a gorgeous stand of pillar coral, its tiny hairs waving in the surge. Back on the sandy plain, look for stingrays, frequently buried in the sand with only their eyes peeking out, as well as colonies of jawfish.

48 Marilyn's Cut (Hole In the Wall)

Two deep canyons cut into the reef, forming dramatic swim-throughs on this section of Bloody Bay Wall, just west of Mixing Bowl.

You'll drop off the wall at about 30ft and descend into a steep canyon-like structure. The sponge life here is magnificent, with nice yellow tube and trumpet sponges and bright-red rope and cup sponges. Make your way around the right side of the huge mass of coral that looks

Location: Bloody Bay

Depth Range: 35-100ft (11-30m)

Access: Boat

Expertise Rating: Intermediate

like it's been cut off from the wall. Look for a steep tunnel—the "hole"—running

Nassau grouper know they have nothing to fear in the marine parks.

PIERCE & NEWMAN

MICHAEL LAWRENCE

Yellow tube and red rope sponges lend the Cayman reefs vibrant color.

parallel to the wall. It winds around a bit and is a lot of fun to explore.

Even if you've encountered really friendly fish before, you won't believe the Nassau grouper that has been hang-ing out here for about 10 years. It will let you and every diver in your group stroke it gently. After spending some time with this guy, you'll never want to eat grouper again.

49 Randy's Gazebo (Chimney)

This dive is like looking down from the top floor of a skyscraper and wondering what it would be like to jump—only now, you can! You can soar right over an incredibly vertical face. Also impressive is the amount of healthy growth on the wall. The barrel sponges are particularly massive. At first glance, you'll feel like a shrunken Alice in Wonderland. You'll

Location: Bloody Bay

Depth Range: 30-100ft (9-30m)

Access: Boat

Expertise Rating: Intermediate

also find plenty of small stuff, such as the yellow-tipped white anemones waving in the surge.

To begin the dive, you descend the "chimney" at 40ft and exit on the face of the wall at 75ft—a thrilling drop. Be careful of the strong current that often runs along the wall, especially where the wall curves inward quite dramatically. At one point the C-shaped curve is so broad that you can fin through blue water for several minutes before you reach the other side.

Toward the end of the deep wall section you'll come across a magnifi-cent photo opportunity—a striking archway in a coral outcropping. The archway makes a perfect frame for a photo of a diver or fish hovering in the blue water.

PIERCE & MORRISEY

Precipitous drop-offs attract divers to Bloody Bay Marine Park.

Just beyond, a massive barrel sponge occupies the point farthest from the wall, standing alone in the blue water. All along this wall are clusters of gorgeous yellow tube sponges. Back in the shallows, you're likely to see black durgon, green turtles, some butterflyfish, but not many schooling fish.

50 Great Wall East & West

Located on the west end of the Bloody Bay Marine Park, this section of wall will likely take your breath away. It features a truly 90-degree drop and in some locations the wall is actually undercut because of protruding growth near the top. It's not a place you want to drop your new camera, so be sure to tether all your loose equipment for these dives.

The area's prolific coral and sponge communities include black coral in the

Location: Bloody Bay

Depth Range: 35-100ft (11-30m)

Access: Boat

Expertise Rating: Intermediate

60ft range. Small reef fish are plentiful, as are black durgon, grouper, eagle rays,

STEVE ROSENBERG

An azure vase sponge reaches out from a crevice in the wall.

horse-eye jacks, yellow jacks and turtles. If you're lucky, you might see an occasional reef shark anywhere along this wall.

The top of the wall is shallow—35 to 40ft—so these areas are fine for less-experienced divers. Brown tube sponges bulge out over the brilliant white sand. Look for sailfin blennies that might pop out of their holes and scorpionfish disguised on coral mounds.

Clipology

Never heard of it? It's the science of clipping off dive gear. And it's important. To protect the reefs, be sure to clip off your octopus and gauges—don't leave anything dangling. Remember, also, that these walls are *very* deep. When you're wall diving, be sure to attach your light, slates, cameras, etc. to a cord or lanyard because if you drop anything it'll be *hasta la bye-bye* to your expensive gear.

51 Coconut Wall (Coconut Grove)

This spectacular site at the west end of Bloody Bay Wall is an extension of the main wall and has similar cuts and canyons. Unlike on the main wall, the extension has two shelves—one is a sort of mini-wall at 30ft and the other is the main wall starting at 60ft.

When you first descend, look for a beautiful stand of pillar coral at about 30ft. You might see stingrays and turtles

Location: Bloody Bay

Depth Range: 30-100ft (9-30m)

Access: Boat

Expertise Rating: Intermediate

STEVE ROSENBERG

here, as well as angelfish and parrotfish. Though most divers see the dark-brown southern stingray in the Caymans, the yellow stingray is also fairly common. It's actually a yellowish-brown and is covered with dark spots. As you make your way over the wall, don't be surprised to see black-tip reef sharks in the cobalt blue beyond. Barrel sponges here are enormous and make good photo subjects.

The polyps of pillar coral are exposed both day and night.

52 Barracuda Bite

Don't worry, this bite is benign—the site probably received its name from a big missing chunk on the face of the reef, where a sandy flow has tumbled over. The structure of this westernmost end of Bloody Bay Wall is interesting, with coral outcroppings extending from the wall. Mountainous star coral reigns supreme here and appears in varied forms.

Location: Bloody Bay

Depth Range: 30-100ft (9-30m)

Access: Boat

Expertise Rating: Intermediate

Take the shallow swim-through out to the edge of the wall and keep a sharp eye on the blue water for turtles and free-swimming—and huge!—moray eels. It's impressive to see them pro- pelling their massive bodies along in the water column. The schooling fish are prolific, as yellowtail snapper seem to compete for space with bluestriped grunts.

PIERCE & NEWMAN

53 Patty's Place

On these south side sites, spur-and-groove formations are the norm, making navigation very easy. Just follow the line of sand out to the main wall and tumble right over. If you're good on air and don't mind diving deep, a beautiful cut in the wall at 120ft makes for dramatic photography. The crevice is narrow at the beginning, then opens up as you near the edge of the wall.

After absorbing a whopping dose of nitrogen, move back up along the wall and you might see cascades of blue chromis soaring over and around overhanging pinnacles. Yellow and green

Location: Preston Bay

Depth Range: 65-120ft (20-40m)

Access: Boat

Expertise Rating: Advanced

tube sponges decorate the face. Remember that the top of the wall is deeper on this side—about 60ft—so be sure to allow yourself plenty of time for your safety stop. While you're gassing off look for jawfish in the rocky rubble.

Navigation Tips for the Caymans

How do those divemasters find their way back to the boat so easily? Here are a few tricks of the trade:

- First, note your depth when you begin the dive, then find the position of the sun and look for natural landmarks.

- If you're diving spur-and-groove coral formations, simply follow one spur out (they extend from the shoreline to the wall) and follow the same spur back again to the boat. Or, count the number of coral fingers you swim over, then count the same number back, making sure you're at the same depth as when you started.

- If you're diving along a wall, note the natural landmarks as you kick out to the drop-off and as you drop down. Definitely use your compass. When ascending, you can swim along the wall until you locate these landmarks again. Or, swim perpendicular to the wall until you reach the same depth you were at the beginning of the dive, then swim parallel to the wall at that depth and you should find the boat.

A pre-dive briefing on Grand Cayman's East End.

PIERCE & NEWMAN

54 Richard's Reef

In these shallows on the south side you'll have a great opportunity to take your time and observe all the underwater action. This is spur-and-groove country, with long coral fingers reaching seaward. Patch reefs are just beyond. Lobster and crab like to retreat under the overlapping star-coral ledges that hang over the sandy thoroughfares.

Location: Preston Bay

Depth Range: 40-60ft (12-18m)

Access: Boat

Expertise Rating: Novice

Search for stingrays in the sandy flats. Also, look for filefish among the gorgonians. Unfortunately, filefish tend to be skittish. Watch for the scrawled variety, which is covered with blue spots, or a dark brownish-yellow variety called the whitespotted filefish. They may or may not have white spots.

The whitespotted filefish during its whitespotted phase.

55 Gay's Reef

Spur-and-groove coral reefs offer a nice opportunity to observe two separate habitats—one in the sand and one on the reef. At this site, there's always a lot going on in both environments. A prolific amount of elkhorn coral grows in the shallows, and schools of jacks or grunts typically hang in formation under the

Location: Preston Bay

Depth Range: 30-60ft (9-18m)

Access: Boat

Expertise Rating: Novice

The spotted trunkfish likes to keep its distance.

beautiful "antlers." You'll also see large patches of staghorn coral a little deeper.

Odds are good for spotting a stingray rooting around in the sand for crustaceans. Goatfish and trunkfish also typically forage in sandy areas. Take time to search for some of the little critters that often get overlooked on those nitro-loading wall dives.

56 Wind Sock Reef

Look toward the shore and you'll be able to see the airport's wind sock from here. This is beautiful shallow spur-and-groove diving, which is a lot of fun especially if you have a camera. You'll probably want a macro lens. Be sure to look underneath the ledges created by overhanging plate coral. Filefish are common here but you'll have to approach them cautiously. You'll probably see balloonfish and conies as well. Check for

Location: Preston Bay

Depth Range: 30-60ft (9-18m)

Access: Boat

Expertise Rating: Novice

conch tracks in the sand—follow them to find the mollusc with the beautiful shell.

A stingray hovers over the sand, sucking up its meal with vacuum-cleaner efficiency.

STEVE ROSENBERG

STEVE ROSENBERG

Nighttime is the right time to explore many of the Caymans' active reefs.

Marine Life

PIERCE & MORRISEY

Marine life in the Cayman Islands is as abundant as it is beautiful. Strict regulations regarding fishing, hunting and collecting mean that the marine creatures here tend to have little fear of divers. If you approach slowly and cautiously with a minimal amount of finning, you can often get surprisingly close. At many sites you'll encounter "friendly" fish—fish that are notably unafraid and curious—especially grouper and angelfish.

The following is a sampling of the common fish and invertebrates you are likely to see in the Caymans, including a photo, common name and scientific name for each. Following that, you will find photos and descriptions for potentially hazardous marine life that you may encounter in Cayman waters. One note on classification and nomenclature: Common names are used freely but are notoriously inaccurate and inconsistent. The two-part scientific name, usually shown in italics, is more precise. It consists of a genus name followed by a species name. A genus is a group of closely related species that share common features. A species is a recognizable group within a genus whose members are capable of interbreeding.

Common Vertebrates

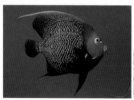

French angelfish
Pomacanthus paru

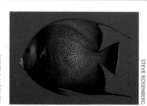

gray angelfish
Pomacanthus arcuatus

queen angelfish
Holacanthus ciliaris

balloonfish
Diodon holocanthus

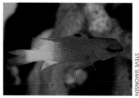

fairy basslet (royal gramma)
Gramma loreto

sailfin blenny
Emblemaria pandionis

foureye butterflyfish
Chaetodon capistratus

coney
Epinephelus fulvus

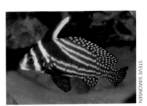

spotted drum
Equetus punctatus

black durgon
Melichthys niger

brown garden eel
Heteroconger halis

whitespotted filefish
Cantherhines macrocerus

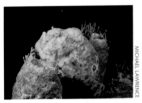

longlure frogfish
Antennarius multiocellatus

Nassau grouper
Epinephelus striatus

bluestriped grunt
Haemulon sciurus

indigo hamlet
Hypoplectrus indigo

hogfish
Lachnolaimus maximus

bar jack
Caranx ruber

yellowhead jawfish
Opistognathus aurifrons

stoplight parrotfish
Sparisoma viride

rock beauty
Holacanthus tricolor

schoolmaster
Lutjanus apodus

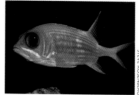

squirrelfish
Holocentrus rufus

blue tang
Acanthurus coeruleus

queen triggerfish
Balistes vetula

spotted trunkfish
Lactophrys bicaudalis

trumpetfish
Aulostomus maculatus

Common Invertebrates

giant anemone
Condylactis gigantea

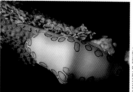

brittle star
Ophiothrix suensonii

elkhorn coral
Acropora palmata

pillar coral
Dendrogyra cylindrus

flamingo tongue
Cyphoma gibbosum

common sea fan
Gorgonia ventalina

sea whip
Elisellidae

orange elephant ear sponge
Agelas clathrodes

vase sponge
Demospongiae

Hazardous Marine Life

Marine animals almost never attack divers, but many have defensive and offensive weaponry that can be triggered if they feel threatened or annoyed. The ability to recognize hazardous creatures is a valuable asset in avoiding accident and injury. The following are some of the potentially hazardous creatures most commonly found in the Cayman Islands:

Barracuda

Barracuda are identifiable by their long, silver, cylindrical bodies and razor-like teeth protruding from an underslung jaw. They swim alone or in small groups, continually opening and closing their mouths, an action that looks daunting, but actually assists their respiration. Though barracuda will hover near divers to observe, they are really somewhat shy, though they may be attracted by shiny objects that resemble fishing lures. Treat a barracuda bite with antiseptics, anti-tetanus and antibiotics.

Moray Eels

Distinguished by their long, thick, snake-like bodies and tapered heads, moray eels come in a variety of colors and patterns. Don't feed them or put your hand in a dark hole—eels have the unfortunate combination of sharp teeth and poor eyesight and will bite if they feel threatened. If you are bitten, don't try to pull your hand away suddenly—the teeth slant backward and are extraordinarily sharp. Let the eel release it and then surface slowly. Treat with antiseptics, anti-tetanus and antibiotics.

STEVE SIMONSEN

Fire Coral

Fire coral is not true coral, but is actually related to jellyfish. Fire coral grows in a variety of shapes and colors, often in colonies composed of finger-like columns with whitish tips. The entire colony is covered by tiny pores and fine, hair-like projections nearly invisible to the unaided eye. Fire coral may encrust and take the form of a variety of reef structures, which makes it difficult to identify by colony shape. Fire corals "sting" by discharging small, specialized cells called nematocysts. Contact causes a burning sensation that lasts for several minutes and may produce red welts on the skin. Do not rub the area, as you will spread the stinging particles. Cortisone cream can reduce the inflammation and antihistamine cream is good for killing the pain. Serious stings should be treated by a doctor.

PIERCE & NEWMAN

PIERCE & NEWMAN

Sea Urchins

Sea urchins tend to live in shallow areas near shore and come out of their shelters at night. They vary in coloration and size, with spines ranging from blunt to needle-sharp. The spines are the urchin's most dangerous weapon, easily able to penetrate neoprene wetsuits, booties and gloves. Treat minor punctures by extracting the spines, immersing in non-scalding hot water. More serious injuries require medical attention.

Scorpionfish

Scorpionfish are well-camouflaged creatures that have poisonous dorsal spines hidden among their fins. They are often difficult to spot since they typically rest quietly on the bottom or on coral, looking more like rocks. Practice good buoyancy control and watch where you put your hands. Scorpionfish wounds can be excruciating. To treat a puncture, wash the wound and immerse in nonscalding hot water for 30 to 90 minutes. Administer pain medications if necessary.

STEVE ROSENBERG

Sharks

Sharks come in many shapes and sizes. They are most recognizable by their triangular dorsal fin. Though many species are shy, there are occasional attacks. About 25 species worldwide are considered dangerous to humans. Sharks will generally not attack unless provoked, so don't

STEVE ROSENBERG

taunt, tease or feed them. Avoid spearfishing, carrying fish baits or mimicking a wounded fish and your likelihood of being attacked will greatly diminish. Face and quietly watch any shark that is acting aggressively and be prepared to push it away with camera, knife or tank. If someone is bitten by a shark, stop the bleeding, reassure the patient, treat for shock and seek immediate medical aid.

STEVE SIMONSEN

Touch-Me-Not Sponge

They may be beautiful, but sponges can pack a powerful punch with fine spicules that sting on contact. Red sponges often carry the most potent sting, although they are not the only culprits. If you touch a stinging sponge, do not rub the area. Remove visible spicules with tweezers, adhesive tape, rubber cement or a commercial facial peel. Soak in vinegar for 10 to 15 minutes. The pain usually goes away within a day. Cortisone cream can help.

Stingrays

Identified by its diamond-shaped body and wide "wings," the stingray has one or two venomous spines at the base of its tail. Although the stingray encounter at Stingray City is a part of most divers' itineraries, it is important that you treat stingrays at other sites differently. Stingrays like shallow waters and tend to rest on silty or sandy bottoms, often burying themselves in the sand. Often only the eyes, gill slits and tail are visible. Generally, these creatures are harmless unless you sit or step on them. Though injuries are uncommon, wounds are always extremely painful, and often deep and infective. Immerse wound in nonscalding hot water, administer pain medications and seek medical aid.

PIERCE & NEWMAN

STEVE ROSENBERG

Diving Conservation & Awareness

The Cayman Islands' phenomenal success as a diving mecca is due primarily to nature—its dramatic underwater topography and abundant marine life thrill divers endlessly. Nevertheless, a great deal of credit must go to those visionaries who worked to preserve and protect the reefs, promoting environmentalism as an important way to attract and retain dive tourism.

Environmental awareness came early to the Cayman Islands and serious conservation efforts began with the formation of the Cayman Islands Watersports Operators Association (CIWOA) in 1982. Its members—dive and watersports operators—assist the Department of the Environment in enforcing marine conservation laws. Protecting the fragile reef systems—and, consequently, the survival of the industry itself—is the primary mission of the organization.

Today, the Department of the Environment maintains a system of permanent public moorings. These moorings are essential to sustainable diving because they prevent the reef damage caused by repeated anchoring.

Also, the Cayman Islands has a strong conservation awareness program as a result of a marine management system established through legislation in 1986. This conservation system established three types of protective zones—Marine Parks, Replenishment Zones and Environmental Zones. Each zone has a specific set of regulations and restrictions.

PIERCE & NEWMAN

Environmental awareness has top priority on Little Cayman.

108

Marine Conservation Zones

In 1986, conservation legislation was introduced, establishing a three-tier system of marine zones with a hierarchy of protective restrictions:

- In **Marine Parks**, only fishing by line from the shore or drop-off onward is allowed, as is the taking of fry by hand net. Boats under 60ft (18m) may only anchor in sand.
- In **Replenishment Zones**, conch or lobster removal is prohibited, but line fishing, anchoring and the taking of fry by hand net are permitted.
- In **Environmental Zones**, the removal of any marine life, alive or dead, is prohibited; anchoring or in-water activities are not permitted; boats are restricted to 5mph (8km/h).

In all zones, fish traps, seine nets and spearguns are banned.

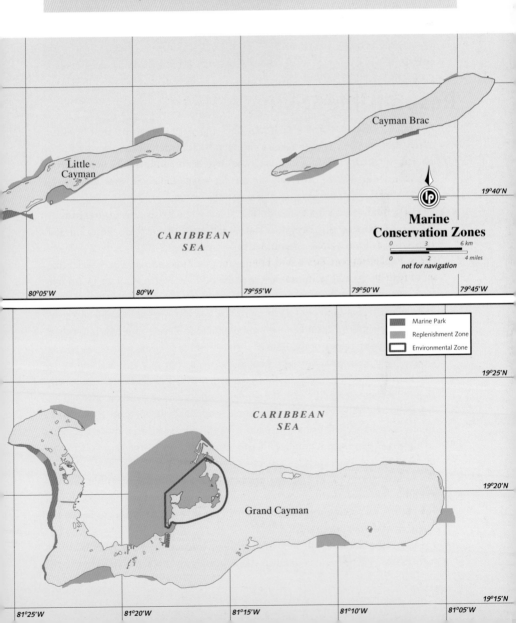

Spearfishing and lobstering with scuba gear is prohibited throughout the Cayman Islands. Taking any marine life while on scuba is also against the law. You may collect shells only on the beach. Many operators discourage divers from wearing gloves. Marine conservation laws are strictly enforced and violations carry severe penalties.

Responsible Diving

Dive sites tend to be located where the reefs and walls display the most beautiful corals and sponges. It only takes a moment—an inadvertently placed hand or knee, or a careless brush or kick with a fin—to destroy this fragile, living part of our delicate ecosystem. By following certain basic guidelines while diving, you can help preserve the ecology and beauty of the reefs:

1. Never drop boat anchors onto a coral reef and take care not to ground boats on coral. Encourage dive operators and regulatory bodies in their efforts to establish permanent moorings at appropriate dive sites.

2. Practice and maintain proper buoyancy control and avoid over-weighting. Be aware that buoyancy can change over the period of an extended trip. Initially you may breathe harder and need more weighting; a few days later you may breathe more easily and need less weight. Tip: Use your weight belt and tank position to maintain a horizontal position–raise them to elevate your feet, lower them to elevate your upper body. Also be careful about buoyancy loss—as you go deeper, your wetsuit compresses, as does the air in your BC.

3. Avoid touching living marine organisms with your body and equipment. Polyps can be damaged by even the gentlest contact. Never stand on or touch living coral. The use of gloves is no longer recommended: gloves make it too easy to hold on to the reef. The abrasion caused by gloves may be even more damaging to the reef than your hands are. If you must hold on to the reef, touch only exposed rock or dead coral.

4. Take great care in underwater caves. Spend as little time within them as possible, as your air bubbles can damage fragile organisms. Divers should take turns inspecting the interior of small caves or under ledges to lessen the chances of damaging contact.

5. Be conscious of your fins. Even without contact, the surge from heavy fin strokes near the reef can do damage. Avoid full-leg kicks when diving close to the

bottom and when leaving a photo scene. When you inadvertently kick something, stop kicking! It seems obvious, but some divers either panic or are totally oblivious when they bump something. When treading water in shallow reef areas, take care not to kick up clouds of sand. Settling sand can smother the delicate reef organisms.

6. Secure gauges, computer consoles and octopus regulators so they're not dangling—they are like miniature wrecking balls to a reef.

7. When swimming in strong currents, be extra careful about leg kicks and handholds.

8. Photographers should take precautions as cameras and equipment affect buoyancy. Changing f-stops, framing a subject and maintaining position for a photo often conspire to prohibit the ideal "no-touch" approach on a reef. When you must use "holdfasts," choose them intelligently (i.e., use one finger only for leverage off an area of dead coral).

9. Resist the temptation to collect or buy coral or shells. Aside from the ecological damage, taking home marine souvenirs depletes the beauty of a site and spoils other divers' enjoyment.

10. Ensure that you take home all your trash and any litter you may find as well. Plastics in particular pose a serious threat to marine life.

11. Resist the temptation to feed fish. You may disturb their normal eating habits, encourage aggressive behavior or feed them food that is detrimental to their health.

12. Minimize your disturbance of marine animals. Don't ride on the backs of turtles or manta rays as this can cause them great anxiety.

Marine Conservation Organizations

Coral reefs and oceans are facing unprecedented environmental pressures. The following groups are actively involved in promoting responsible diving practices, publicizing environmental marine threats and lobbying for better policies.

Project AWARE Foundation
☎ 714-540-0251
www.projectaware.org

CEDAM International
☎ 914-271-5365
www.cedam.org
cedamint@aol.com

CORAL: The Coral Reef Alliance
☎ 510-848-0110
www.coral.org

Coral Forest
☎ 415-788-REEF
www.blacktop.com/coralforest/index.html

Cousteau Society
☎ 757-523-9335
www.cousteau.org

ReefKeeper International
☎ 305-358-4600
www.reefkeeper.org

Listings

Telephone Calls

The area code for all three islands is 345 and all local telephone numbers have seven digits. To call from the U.S., Canada, Bermuda and within the Caribbean, dial 1 + 345 + the local number. From elsewhere, use the country's international access code + 1 + 345 + the local number. Toll-free numbers can be reached from most U.S. and Canadian cities.

Accommodations

The following lodgings are appropriate for divers. Other than the condos, they all have dive operations on the premises and offer dive and lodging packages.

Grand Cayman

Beach Club Hotel & Dive Resort (41 rooms)
Seven Mile Beach
☎ 949-8100 fax: 945-5167
Toll-free: 800-482-3483
cayresv@candw.ky
Dive Service: Beach Club Dive Shop

Cayman Diving Lodge (10 rooms)
East End, south side
☎ 947-7555 fax: 947-7560
Toll-free: 800-852-3483
divelodge@aol.com
Dive Service: Cayman Divers

Coconut Harbour (35 rooms)
South Church St., southern George Town
☎ 949-7468 fax: 949-7117
Toll-free: 800-552-6281
Dive Service: Parrot's Landing

Indies Suites (41 suites)
Seven Mile Beach
☎ 945-5025 fax: 945-5024
Toll-free: 800-654-3130
indiessuites@worldnet.att.net
Dive Service: Red Sail Sports

Morritt's Tortuga Club & Resort (169 rooms)
East End
☎ 947-7449 fax: 947-7299

Toll-free: 800-447-0309
reservations@morritts.com
Dive Service: Tortuga Divers

Seaview Hotel (15 rooms)
Seven Mile Beach
☎ 945-0558 fax: 945-0559
seadive@candw.ky
Dive Service: Seaview Dive Center

Sleep Inn Hotel (115 rooms)
Seven Mile Beach
☎ 949-9111 fax: 949-6699
Toll-free: 800-753-3746
sleepinn@candw.ky
Dive Service: Treasure Island Divers

Sunset House (59 rooms)
South Church St., southern George Town
☎ 949-7111 fax: 949-7101
Toll-free: 800-854-4767
sunseth@candw.ky
www.sunsethouse.com
Dive Service: Sunset Divers

Treasure Island Resort (278 rooms)
Seven Mile Beach
☎ 949-7777 fax: 949-8489
Toll-free: 800-203-0775
Dive Service: Scuba Sensation

Grand Cayman - Condos & Villas

Caribbean Club (18 villas)
Seven Mile Beach
☎ 945-4099 fax: 945-4443
caribclub@cayman.org

Discovery Point Club (45 condos)
Seven Mile Beach
☎ 945-4724 fax:945-5051
discoverypoint@cayman.org

Seagull Condominiums (32 condos)
Seven Mile Beach
☎ 949-5756 fax: 949-9040
seagull@cayman.org

Silver Sands Condominiums (42 condos)
West Bay Rd.
☎ 949-3343 fax: 949-1223
Toll-free: 800-327-8777 (U.S.),
800-424-5500 (Canada)
silversands@cayman.org

Villas of the Galleon (60 villas)
Seven Mile Beach
☎ 945-4433 fax: 945-4705
galleon@cayman.org

Cayman Brac

Brac Reef Beach Resort (40 rooms)
West End, south side
☎ 948-1323 fax: 948-1207
Toll-free: 800-327-3835
bestdiving@aol.com
Dive Service: Reef Divers

Brac Caribbean Beach Village (40 condos)
Stake Bay
☎ 948-2265 fax: 948-1111
bracarib@candw.ky
Dive Service: Brac Aquatics

Carib Sands (30 condos)
Stake Bay
☎ 948-1121 fax: 948-1122
caribsan@candw.ky

Divi Tiara Beach Resort (71 rooms)
Stake Bay
☎ 948-1553 fax: 948-1316
Toll-free: 800-367-3484
stevo@candw.ky
Dive Service: Dive Tiara

Little Cayman

Conch Club Condominiums (12 condos)
Blossom Village
☎ 948-1033 fax: 948-1040
Toll-free: 800-327-3835
conchclub@aol.com
www.conchclub.com
Dive Service: Conch Club Divers

Little Cayman Beach Resort (40 rooms)
Blossom Village
☎ 948-1033 fax: 948-1014
Toll-free: 800-327-3835
LCBR@candw.ky
www.littlecayman.com
Dive Service: Reef Divers

Paradise Villas (12 villas)
Blossom Village
☎ 948-0001 fax: 948-0002
iggy@candw.ky
Dive Service: Paradise Divers

Pirate's Point Resort (10 rooms)
Preston Bay
☎ 948-1010 fax: 948-1011
Dive Service: Pirate's Point Divers

Sam McCoy's Diving & Fishing Lodge
(8 rooms)
North Side, west end
☎ 948-0026 fax: 948-0026
Toll-free: 800-626-0496
mccoy@candw.ky
www.cayman.com.ky/com/sam
Dive Service: Sam McCoy's Divers

Southern Cross Club (11 rooms)
South Hole Sound
☎ 949-1099 fax: 949-1098
Toll-free: 800-899-2582
relax@southerncrossclub.com
www.southerncrossclub.com
Dive Service: Southern Cross Club Divers

Dining

The following is a variety of recommended independent restaurants, most of which have moderate prices. You will also find excellent restaurants and cafés at the resorts, but these tend to be more expensive.

Grand Cayman

Almond Tree
North Church St., George Town
☎ 949-2893
Caribbean seafood; outdoor patio

Bed Restaurant & Lounge
Islander Complex, West Bay Rd.
☎ 949-7199
Fine dining

Champion House I & II
Eastern Ave., George Town
☎ 949-7882
Local specialties

Crow's Nest
South Sound, on the beach

☎ 949-9366
Caribbean seafood; beach view

Eat's Crocodile Rock Café
Cayman Falls Centre, West Bay Rd.
☎ 945-5288
American-style diner

Edoardo's
Coconut Place, West Bay Rd.
☎ 945-4408
Seafood, pasta & pizza

Lone Star Bar & Grille
West Bay Rd., near the Hyatt
☎ 945-5175
Tex-Mex specialties

Cayman Brac

Aunt Sha's Kitchen
West End
☎ 948-1581
Local seafood dishes

Captain's Table
Stake Bay, Brac Caribbean Beach Village

☎ 948-1418
Fine dining

La Esperanza
North Road, East End
☎ 948-0531
Seafood, outdoor-grilled jerk chicken

Little Cayman

Hungry Iguana Restaurant & Bar
Blossom Village
☎ 948-0007
Large selection, occasional live entertainment

Diving Services

The following dive operations are well established and reliable. Most are members of the Cayman Islands Watersports Operators Association.

Grand Cayman

Ambassador Divers
Box 2396 GT
South Church St., George Town
☎ 949-8839 fax: 945-8838
ambadive@candw.ky
Sales: Limited **Rentals:** Full, including cameras & videoscooters
Air: On-site fills; nitrox available
Boats: 28ft Parker (12 max.)
Trips: Daily 2-tank dives on North, West & South Walls; Stingray City; snorkel trips
Courses: BSAC, PADI beginner through divemaster, specialty courses
Other: Courtesy shuttle

Aquanauts
Box 30147 SMB
Morgan's Harbour, West Bay
☎ 945-1990 fax: 945-1991
sales@worlddive.com
www.worlddive.com
Sales & Rentals: Full
Air: On-site air & nitrox fills
Boats: 2 custom V hulls: 42ft & 50ft
Trips: Daily 1- & 2-tank dives on North & West Walls
Courses: IDEA, NASDS, NAUI, PADI, SSI beginner through advanced, nitrox, rebreather, photo/video
Other: Courtesy shuttle; jet-boat rentals & boat charters

Bob Soto's Diving
Box 1801 GT
North Church St., George Town
☎ 949-2022 fax: 949-8731
bobsotos@candw.ky
www.bobsotosdiving.com.ky
Sales & Rentals: Full; camera rental at Treasure Island location
Air: On-site fills; nitrox available
Boats: 7 boats, all custom outfitted; 20-passenger 59ft, 46ft, 42ft, 40ft & 39ft; 14-passenger 35ft; 3 12- & 16-passengers 32ft vessels; 4-passenger 17ft
Trips: Daily 1-, 2- & 3-tank dives to North, West & South Walls, East End Safari, Stingray City
Courses: PADI 5-Star Development & Training Center, beginner through instructor
Other: 4 locations: Treasure Island Resort, The Strand Shopping Center, Coconuts Shopping Center, the Lobster Pot; photo center at Treasure Island Resort; shore diving at the Lobster Pot

Capt. Marvin's
Box 413 WB
Coconut Place, West Bay Rd., George Town
☎ 945-4590 fax: 945-5673
captmvn@candw.ky
www.padi.com/dive/captainmarvins/home.htm
Sales: None **Rentals:** BC & regulator
Air: Off-site fills
Boats: 6 cabin cruisers, 28ft to 43ft
Trips: Daily 1- & 2-tank dives & snorkeling to shallow sites, Stingray City; full-day trips
Courses: PADI beginner through advanced; snorkel class
Other: Courtesy shuttle

Cayman Diving Lodge
Box 11 EE
East End
☎ 947-7555 fax: 947-7560
caymandivelodge@cayman.org
www.divelodge.com
Sales & Rentals: Full, including cameras & video
Air: On-site fills
Boats: Pro 48, 45ft Garcia
Trips: Daily 2- & 3-tank dives, night dives
Courses: PADI beginner through divemaster, specialty courses, nitrox
Other: Dedicated diving lodge, courtesy shuttle

Dive 'n Stuff
Box 30609 SMB
North Church St., George Town
☎ 949-6033 fax: 945-9207
divenstuff@cayman.org
www.cayman.org/divenstuff/
Sales & Rentals: Full, including cameras & video
Air: On-site fills; nitrox available
Boats: Custom 12-passenger 28ft tri-hull pontoon
Trips: Daily 2-tank dives on West End
Courses: PADI beginner through assistant instructor
Other: Courtesy shuttle, custom trips, charters, videos

Grand Cayman (continued)

Divers Down
Box 1706 GT
West Bay Rd., George Town
☎ 945-1611 fax: 945-1611
andyp@candw.ky
www.cayman.org/diversdown
Sales: None **Rentals:** Full
Air: Off-site fills; nitrox available
Boats: 3 8-passenger boats
Trips: Daily 1 & 2-tank dives, night dives, Stingray City
Courses: PADI beginner through assistant instructor

Divers Supply
Box 1995 GT
West Shore Centre
West Bay Rd., George Town
☎ 949-7621 fax: 949-7616
Diversup@candw.ky
Sales & Rentals: Full, including cameras & technical gear
Air: Off-site fills; nitrox available
Trips: Trips booked with Parrot's Landing
Other: Equipment service

Divetech
Box 31435 SMB
North West Point, West Bay
☎ 949-1700 fax: 949-1701
divetech@candw.ky
www.divetech.com
Sales & Rentals: Full, including rebreathers, twin & deco tanks, scooters, metal detectors, communications equipment, cameras
Air: Blending station; nitrox blends, oxygen & mixes for technical diving
Boats: 10-passenger 34ft Delta
Trips: Daily 1- & 2-tank dives on North Wall & Northwest Point; technical trips; free-diving & snorkel trips; night dives
Courses: BSAC, IANTD, MDEA, NASDS, NAUI, PADI, PDIC, SSI, TDI, YMCA beginner through instructor; also nitrox, advanced nitrox, technical nitrox, trimix, rebreather; free-diving certification, snorkeling
Other: Technical diving playground & center for free-diving; shore diving; courtesy shuttle; apartment rentals

Don Foster's Dive Cayman
Box 31486 SMB
George Town Harbour
☎ 945-5132 fax: 945-5133
donfosters@cayman.org

www.cayman.org/donfosters/
Sales & Rentals: Full
Air: On-site fills; nitrox available
Boats: 59ft & 2 52ft custom-built flat-tops; custom-built 42ft V-hull; 65ft twin deck catamaran
Trips: Daily 1- & 2-tank dives, night dives, Stingray City, snorkel excursions
Courses: PADI beginner through dive-master, specialty courses
Other: Shore diving on *Cali* wreck; sunset & dinner cruises

Eden Rock Diving Center
Box 1907 GT
South Church St., George Town
☎ 949-7243 fax: 949-0842
edenrock@candw.ky
Sales & Rentals: Full, including camera & video rentals
Air: On-site fills; nitrox available
Boats: Pro 42
Trips: Daily 1- & 2-tank dives to North, South & West Walls, 3-tank North Wall dives with lunch, night dives, Stingray City
Courses: BSAC, NAUI, PADI, SSI beginner through advanced, specialty courses
Other: Shore diving, lockers, photo center, service & repairs

Fisheye
Box 30076 SMB
West Bay Rd., Seven Mile Beach
☎ 945-4209 fax: 945-4208
fisheye@candw.ky
www.fisheye.com
Sales: Full **Rentals:** Full, including cameras, video & housings
Air: Off-site fills; nitrox available
Boats: 3 custom boats, 36ft pontoon, 31ft V-hull
Trips: Daily 1- & 2-tank dives, night dives, Stingray City
Courses: Courses through Divetech, nitrox, photo
Other: Custom photographs, slide processing, camera repairs

Ocean Frontiers
Box 30433 SMB
Church St., On East End
☎ 947-7500 fax: 947-7600
oceanf@candw.ky
www.oceanfrontiers.com
Sales: None **Rentals:** Full, including cameras & video

Grand Cayman (continued)

Air: On-site fills; nitrox available
Boats: 38ft custom catamaran
Trips: Daily 1- & 2-tank dives on East End, night dives, Stingray City, reef snorkel trips
Courses: PADI beginner through advanced, nitrox, rebreather, photo & video
Other: Courtesy shuttle, charters

Parrot's Landing Watersports Park
Box 1995 GT
South Church St., George Town
☎ 949-7884 fax: 949-0294
parrots@candw.ky
www.parrotslanding.com
Sales: Full **Rentals:** Full, including cameras & video
Air: On-site fills; nitrox available
Boats: 2 custom 45ft dive boats & racing catamaran
Trips: Daily 2-tank dives on North Wall, Northwest Point, West & South Walls, 1-tank Stingray City dives, 3-tank safari & lunch, night dives; sailing & snorkeling on *Cockatoo* catamaran
Courses: NAUI, PADI, SSI beginner through rescue, specialty courses
Other: Photo center, camera repair; shore diving; hotel/condo packages

Peter Milburn's Dive Cayman
Box 596 GT
Seven Mile Beach
☎ 945-5770 fax: 945-5786
pmilburn@candw.ky
Sales: None **Rentals:** Limited
Air: Off-site fills
Boats: 3 flattop boats: 26ft, 34ft & 36ft
Trips: Morning 2-tank dives, night dives, Stingray City
Courses: Resort course & PADI Open Water checkout dives
Other: No credit cards; baby-sitting services for divers

Quabo Dives
Box 157 GT
Coconut Place, West Bay Rd., George Town
☎ 945-4767 fax: 945-4978
quabo@candw.ky
Sales: None **Rentals:** Full
Air: Off-site fills; nitrox available
Boats: Custom 39-ft dive boat
Trips: Daily 2-tank dives to North, West & South Walls, night dives, Stingray City
Courses: PADI beginner through advanced
Other: Custom videos

Red Sail Sports
Box 31473 SMB
Seven Mile Beach
☎ 945-5965 fax: 945-5808
redsail@candw.ky
www.redsail.com
Sales & Rentals: Full, including cameras & video
Air: On-site fills; nitrox available
Boats: 42ft Newton, 43ft custom boat, 2 46ft custom boats, Pro 51 tri-maran, 35ft Crusader, 2 65ft catamarans for snorkeling
Trips: Daily 1- & 2-tank dives to North Wall, night dives, 3-tank safari, Stingray City, snorkel trips
Courses: NASDS, NAUI, PADI, SSI beginner through divemaster, specialty courses
Other: 4 locations: Hyatt, Westin, Marriott, Rum Point; catamaran cruises, charters

Seaview Dive Center
Box 31900 SMB
South Church St., George Town
☎ 945-0577 fax: 945-0577
seadive@candw.ky
www.diveguideint.com/seaview
Sales: None **Rentals:** Full, including rebreathers
Air: Off-site fills; nitrox available
Boats: 34ft Crusader
Trips: 2-tank boat dives, guided shore dives
Courses: PADI beginner through divemaster, nitrox, rebreather
Other: Shore diving

Sunset Divers
Box 479 GT
South Church St., George Town
☎ 949-7111 fax: 949-7101
sunseths@candw.ky
www.sunsethouse.com
Sales: Full **Rentals:** Full range, including cameras & video
Air: On-site fills; nitrox available
Boats: 6 boats: 2 custom 36ft, also 38ft, 45ft, 12-passenger Crusader, 45ft catamaran
Trips: Daily 2-tank dives to West Coast, North Wall & South Sound, 3-tank manta dives, Stingray City, night dives
Courses: NASDS, NAUI, PADI, SSI beginner through advanced, specialty courses
Other: Shore diving, charters, commercial diving, repairs

Grand Cayman (continued)

Surfside Watersports
Box 30370 SMB
Billy's Place, Seven Mile Beach
☎ 949-7330 fax: 949-8639
surfdive@candw.ky
www.cayman.org/surfside/
Sales: None **Rentals:** Full
Air: Off-site fills; nitrox available
Boats: 42ft Down Under
Trips: Daily 1- & 2-tank dives, 3-tank all-day dive, night dives
Courses: PADI beginner to advanced; nitrox, specialty courses
Other: Courtesy shuttle, group packages & charters

Treasure Island Divers
Box 30975 SMB
Seven Mile Beach
☎ 949-4456 fax: 949-7125
tidivers@netrunner.net
www.tidivers.com
Sales: Full **Rentals:** Full, including cameras & video
Air: On-site fills; nitrox available

Boats: 3 custom-built dive boats
Trips: Daily 2-tank dives, night dives, Stingray City
Courses: PADI beginner to advanced; nitrox, specialties
Other: Photo center, courtesy shuttle

Turtle Reef Divers
Box 30975 SMB
North West Point, West Bay
☎ 949-1700 fax: 949-1701
divetech@candw.ky
www.divetech.com
Sales: Full **Rentals:** Full, including rebreathers, cameras & videoscooters
Air: On-site air, nitrox, other mixes
Boats: 34ft Delta
Trips: Daily 1- & 2-tank dives on North Wall & Northwest Point; technical trips; free-diving & snorkel trips; night dives
Courses: Courses through Divetech, experience rebreather course
Other: Shore diving; courtesy shuttle; apartment rentals

Cayman Brac

Brac Aquatics Dive & Photo Centre
Box 89
Brac Caribbean Beach Village, West End
☎ 948-1429 fax: 948-1527
Sales: Full **Rentals:** Full, including cameras & video
Air: On-site fills; nitrox available
Boats: 55ft Out Runner, 48ft Reef Runner
Trips: Daily 1- & 2-tank dives; 2- & 3-tank dives to Little Cayman 3 times weekly, night dives; snorkel trips
Courses: NAUI, PADI beginner through advanced, photo courses
Other: Shore diving; film processing

Divi Tiara, Peter Hughes
Box 238 STB
Divi Tiara Beach Resort, Stake Bay
☎ 948-1563 fax: 948-1316
divtiara@candw.ky
diviresorts.com
Sales: Full **Rentals:** Full, including cameras & video
Air: On-site air & nitrox fills
Boats: 4 40ft custom boats, 1 38ft
Trips: Daily 1- & 2-tank dives; Little Cayman dives 3 times weekly
Courses: NASDS, NAUI, PADI beginner through divemaster; nitrox (TDI)

Other: Photo center, E-6 processing

Reef Divers
Box 56
Brac Reef Beach Resort, West End
☎ 948-1323 fax: 948-1207
bestdiving@aol.com
www.braclittle.com
Sales: Full **Rentals:** Full, including cameras & video
Air: On-site fills; nitrox available
Boats: 2 Newton 42s, Newton 46, Pro 42
Trips: Daily 1- & 2-tank dives; Little Cayman's Bloody Bay Marine Park
Courses: BSAC, NAUI, PADI, SSI beginner through divemaster, specialty courses
Other: Photo & video center; custom videos

Village Scuba School
Box 206
Brac Caribbean Beach Village, West End
☎ 948-1467 fax: 948-1501
Sales & Rentals: At Brac Aquatics
Courses: PADI beginner through divemaster, many specialties, snorkeling, children's courses
Other: Ecology lectures, slide presentations, tide pool excursions

Little Cayman

Paradise Divers

Box 48
Blossom Village
☎ 948-0001 fax: 948-0002
iggy@candw.ky
www.scubatimes.com
Sales: None **Rentals:** Full
Air: On-site fills; nitrox available
Boats: 2 pontoon boats, 28ft & 43ft
Trips: Daily 2-tank dives, night dives, snorkel & Owen Island trips, sunset cruises
Courses: NAUI, PADI beginner through divemaster

Pirate's Point Resort

Box 43
Preston Bay
☎ 948-1010 fax: 948-1011
Sales: None **Rentals:** Full
Air: On-site fills; nitrox available
Boats: Newton 42
Trips: Daily 2-tank dives, night dives; *Tibbetts* on Cayman Brac
Courses: NAUI, PADI, SSI beginner through advanced, some specialties, nitrox
Other: Snorkeling from property, airport pickup, custom videos

Reef Divers

Box 51
Blossom Village, Little Cayman Beach Resort
☎ 948-1033 fax: 948-1040
reefdive@candw.ky
www.braclittle.com
Sales: Full **Rentals:** Full, including cameras & video
Air: On-site air & nitrox fills

Boats: 3 42ft Newtons
Trips: Daily 1- & 2-tank dives; night dives; *Tibbetts* on Cayman Brac
Courses: IANTD, PADI, TDI beginner through divemaster; nitrox; photo
Other: Photo & video center

Sam McCoys Diving & Fishing Lodge

Box 12 LC
North Side
☎ 948-0026 fax: 948-0057
mccoy@candw.ky
www.cayman.com.ky/com/sam
Sales: None **Rentals:** Full
Air: On-site fills; nitrox available
Boats: 31ft custom dive boat
Trips: Daily 1- & 2-tank dives, night dives, snorkel
Other: Owen Island conching trips, picnic trips

Southern Cross Club

Box 44
South Hole Sound
☎ 948-1099 fax: 948-1098
scc@candw.ky
www.southerncrossclub.com
Sales: None **Rentals:** Limited
Air: On-site fills; nitrox available
Boats: 34ft Crusader, 36ft Sea Hawk
Trips: Daily 1- & 2-tank dives; night dives; *Tibbetts* on Cayman Brac
Courses: PADI beginner through advanced; nitrox (IANTD)
Other: Group rates

Live-Aboards

Cayman Aggressor IV

PO Box 1882 GT
George Town
☎ 949-5551 fax 949-8729
divboat@aol.com
www.aggressor.com
Home Port: George Town
Description: 110ft aluminum dive yacht; 22ft beam, 7ft draft; 9 staterooms
Equipment: Twin generators; twin compressors with cascade storage & nitrox membrane for EANx32; water maker; complete

communications & safety equipment; Atlantis rebreathers
Accommodations: Staterooms have private heads, TV/VCR, climate control; hot tub; photo center with E-6 film processing; guest computer station
Destinations: Grand Cayman's North, West & South Walls; Little Cayman & Cayman Brac
Duration: 7 nights
Season: All year
Passengers: 18

Live-Aboards (continued)

Little Cayman Diver II
PO Box 273781
Tampa, FL 33688
☎ 813-962-2236
wmcdermot@earthlink.net
www.littlecaymandiver.com
Home Port: Cayman Brac
Description: 90ft aluminum dive yacht; 21ft
beam, 7ft draft; 5 staterooms

Equipment: Twin generators; twin compressors; water maker; complete communications & safety equipment
Accommodations: Staterooms have private heads and showers, climate control
Destinations: Little Cayman & Cayman Brac
Duration: 7 nights
Season: All year
Passengers: 10

Cruise Lines

Carnival Cruise Line
Carnival Place
3655 NW 87 Ave.
Miami, FL 33178
☎ 877-810-6600
www.carnival.com
Boats: *Imagination*, home port Miami,
2,634 passengers; *Tropicale*, home port
Tampa, 1,396 passengers; *Paradise*, home
port Miami, 2,600 passengers; *Celebration*,
home port New Orleans, 1,840 passengers;
Sensation, home port Tampa, 2,364 passengers

Celebrity Cruises, Inc.
Marine Operations
1050 Caribbean Way
Miami, FL 33132
☎ 800-789-5106
www.celebritycruises.com
Boats: *Mercury*, home port Miami, 1,870
passengers; *Century*, home port Miami,
1,750 passengers

Costa Cruise Lines
80 SW 8th St.
Miami, FL 33130-3097
☎ 800-462-6782
www.costacruises.com
Boats: *Costa Romantica*, home port Ft.
Lauderdale, 1,600 passengers; *Costa Victoria*, home port Ft. Lauderdale, 2,250
passengers

Holland America Lines
300 Elliott Ave. W
Seattle, WA 98119
☎ 877-724-5425
www.hollandamerica.com
Boats: *Ryndam* and *Veendam*, home port
Ft. Lauderdale, 1,266 passengers each

Norwegian Cruise Lines
7665 Corporate Center Dr.
Miami, FL 33126
www.ncl.com
Boats: *Norwegian*, home port Miami, 1,726
passengers; *The Norway*, home port Miami,
2,032 passengers

Princess Cruises
1801 SE 20th St.
Terminal 2
Ft. Lauderdale, FL 33316
☎ 800-774-2377
www.princesscruises.com
Boats: *Crown Princess*, home port Ft.
Lauderdale, 1,590 passengers; *Sea Princess*,
home port Ft. Lauderdale, 1,950 passengers

Royal Caribbean Cruise Lines
1050 Caribbean Way
Miami, FL 33132
☎ 800-722-5053
www.royalcaribbean.com
Boats: *Enchantment of the Seas*, home port
Miami, 2,446 passengers; *Majesty of the
Seas*, home port Miami, 2,354 passengers;
Splendour of the Seas, home port Miami,
1,804 passengers

Regal Cruises
300 Regal Cruise Way
Palmetto, FL 33334
☎ 800-270-7245
www.regalcruises.com
Boats: MV *Regal Empress*, home port
Tampa Bay, 1,068 passengers

Underwater Photography & Video

Cathy Church's Underwater Photo Centre
Sunset House Hotel
Grand Cayman
☎ 949-7415

Fisheye Diving Photography & Video
Cayman Falls Center, Seven Mile Beach
Grand Cayman
☎ 945-4209

Brac Photographics
Brac Reef Beach Resort
Cayman Brac
☎ 948-1340

Brac Aquatics Dive & Photo Center
Brac Caribbean Beach Village
Cayman Brac
☎ 948-1553

Photo Tiara
Divi Tiara Beach Resort
Cayman Brac
☎ 948-1553

Reef Photo & Video Center
Little Cayman Beach Resort
Little Cayman
☎ 948-1063

Tourist Offices

Cayman Islands Department of Tourism
The Pavillion, Cricket Square
Box 67 GT
George Town, Grand Cayman, BWI
☎ 949-0623 fax: 949-4053
Toll-free: 800-346-3313 for information and reservations
www.caymanislands.ky

Cayman Islands Watersports Operators Association
☎ 949-8522
ciwoa@candw.ky

Cayman National Watersports Association
☎ 949-3200 or ☎ 949-1750

Sister Islands Tourism Association
☎ 948-1649

Index

dive sites covered in this book appear in **bold** type

Lonely Planet Pisces Books

The **Diving & Snorkeling** guides cover top destinations worldwide. Beautifully illustrated with full-color photos throughout, the series explores the best diving and snorkeling areas and prepares divers for what to expect when they get there. Each site is described in detail, with information on suggested ability levels, depth, visibility and, of course, marine life. There's basic topside information as well for each destination.

Also check out dive guides to:

Lonely Planet Series Descriptions

Lonely Planet **travel guides** explore a destination in depth with options to suit a range of budgets. With reliable, practical advice on getting around, restaurants and accommodations, these easy-to-use guides also include detailed maps, color photographs, extensive background material and coverage of sites both on and off the beaten track.

For budget travelers **shoestring guides** are the best single source of travel information covering an entire continent or large region. Written by experienced travelers these 'tried and true' classics offer reliable, first-hand advice on transportation, restaurants and accommodations, and insider tips for avoiding bureaucratic confusion and stretching money as far as possible.

City guides cover many of the world's great cities with full-color photographs throughout, front and back cover gatefold maps, and information for every traveler's budget and style. With information for business travelers, all the best places to eat and shop and itinerary suggestions for long and short-term visitors, city guides are a complete package.

Lonely Planet **phrasebooks** have essential words and phrases to help travelers communicate with the locals. With color tabs for quick reference, an extensive vocabulary, use of local scripts and easy-to-follow pronunciation instructions, these handy, pocket-sized language guides cover most situations a traveler is likely to encounter.

Lonely Planet **walking guides** cover some of the world's most exciting trails. With detailed route descriptions including degrees of difficulty and best times to go, reliable maps and extensive background information, these guides are an invaluable resource for both independent hikers and those in organized groups.

Lonely Planet **travel atlases** are thoroughly researched and fact-checked by the guidebook authors to ensure they complement the books. The handy format means none of the holes, wrinkles, tears or constant folding and refolding of flat maps. They include background information in five languages.

Journeys is a new series of travel literature that captures the spirit of a place, illuminates a culture, recounts an adventure and introduces a fascinating way of life. Written by a diverse group of writers, they are tales to read while on the road or at home in your favorite armchair.

Entertaining, independent and adventurous, Lonely Planet **videos** encourage the same approach to travel as the guidebooks. Currently broadcast throughout the world, this award-winning series features all original footage and music.

Lonely Planet Online

Get the latest travel information before you leave
or while you're on the road

Whether you've just begun planning your next trip, or you're chasing down specific info on currency regulations or visa requirements, check out Lonely Planet Online for up-to-the-minute travel information.

As well as travel profiles of your favorite destinations (including maps and photos), you'll find current reports from our researchers and other travelers, updates on health and visas, travel advisories, and discussion of the ecological and political issues you need to be aware of as you travel.

There's also an online travelers' forum where you can share your experience of life on the road, meet travel companions and ask other travelers for their recommendations and advice. We also have plenty of links to other online sites useful to independent travelers.

And of course we have a complete and up-to-date list of all Lonely Planet travel products including guides, phrasebooks, atlases, Journeys and videos and a simple online ordering facility if you can't find the book you want elsewhere.

www.lonelyplanet.com or AOL keyword: lp

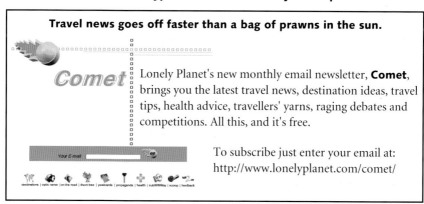

Travel news goes off faster than a bag of prawns in the sun.

Lonely Planet's new monthly email newsletter, **Comet**, brings you the latest travel news, destination ideas, travel tips, health advice, travellers' yarns, raging debates and competitions. All this, and it's free.

To subscribe just enter your email at:
http://www.lonelyplanet.com/comet/

Where to Find Us . . .

Lonely Planet is known worldwide for publishing practical, reliable and no-nonsense travel information in our guides and on our website. The Lonely Planet list covers just about every accessible part of the world. Currently there are nine series: *Pisces books, travel guides, shoestring guides, walking guides, city guides, phrasebooks, audio packs, travel atlases* and *Journeys*–a unique collection of travel writing.

Lonely Planet Publications

Australia
P.O. Box 617, Hawthorn 3122, Victoria
☎ (03) 9819 1877 fax: (03) 9819 6459
email: talk2us@lonelyplanet.com.au

UK
10A Spring Place,
London NW5 3BH
☎ (0171) 428 4800 fax: (0171) 428 4828
email: go@lonelyplanet.co.uk

USA
150 Linden Street
Oakland, California 94607
☎ (510) 893 8555, (800) 275 8555
fax: (510) 893 8563
email: info@lonelyplanet.com

France
1 rue du Dahomey
75011 Paris
☎ 01 55 25 33 00 fax: 01 55 25 33 01
email: bip@lonelyplanet.fr

www.lonelyplanet.com

EAGLE VALLEY LIBRARY DISTRICT
P.O. BOX 240   600 BROADWAY
EAGLE, CO 81631   (970) 328-8800